I Asked for a Rose…
But God Sent an Orchid

By Cindy and Wade
Robinson
As Told to Jo Bower

Copyright 2005
Revised May 2011
by
Jo Bower
DBA
Ten Talents Publishing
147 Hwy 1206, Deville, LA 71328
http://jobowerwrites.wordpress.com

ISBN 0-9721530-4-7 (10 Digit)
978-0-9721530-4-1 (13 Digit)

AS TOLD TO JO BOWER...

Jo Bower is an author and publisher whose published work includes devotional material, fiction and drama. She shares her life with her husband, Monty, who is a pastor, his library, her piano, and various electronic devices. She is also an improvisational scared music pianist and enjoys reading mysteries and spy stories

Jo works as a writer for hire, writes a series of Inspirational Science Fiction Novels, Readers' Plays for small churches, and two person dramas that illustrate scriptures.

Her work is available on Amazon.com and through http://tellsof cutezar.tripod.com. Check in on Jo through her blog: http://jobowerwrites. wordpress.com.

Thanks to the following people:

Jo Bower, author
For writing our story, her patience,
and designing our awesome cover.

Our parents,
Elmer and Jewel Hunsaker
and John and Katie Robinson,
For their love and support and the impact they
made on our lives.

Our children
Marvin, Ken, Dorothy Grace, Sheryl, Dale,
Connie and their spouses,
For teaching us invaluable life's lessons.
Our many relatives, friends, mentors,
and counselors, Who walked alongside us during
the good times and the not so good times.

Rev. Ken Martin,
For "putting his thumb" in my (Cindy) back and
strongly encouraging me to go through the process
of getting my ordination parchments back.

Rev. Charles Kaufmann,
Who faithfully preached God's word in those post-
divorce years. They were life giving to me (Cindy)
and spurred me on to spiritual and personal growth.

Dr. John Williams, "Burn Doctor" and his very competent staff of nurses,

Who took excellent care of me (Wade) and went the second mile in the extensive recovery.

Dorothy Sylvester,

(A nurse at Natchez Regional Hospital)
Who kept after me (Cindy) and encouraged me to write our story.

Julie Bird,

Occupational Therapist, LaSalle General Hospital Who faithfully kept after me (Wade) to call Kansas.

Sharon West,

Occupational Therapist
Who faithfully gave therapy and spent hours listening to my (Wade) story.

Our Siblings

Wade: **Lillian, John and Helen**
(John and Helen are deceased)
Cindy: **Ethelyn, Robert and Lowell**
For walking the journey of life with us, and their loving support and care.

Table Of Contents

Secrets have a way of making their presence felt. We may think we are done with them, having filed them away and forgotten about them. But they are still there, often disguised in a stubborn feeling of unhappiness or uneasiness that refuses to go away.

Secrets are like walls keeping spouses apart. Forever hidden away, our secrets set us apart, keeping who we really are an enigma. Life itself is a secret unfolding.

When we make a sincere and honest disclosure of who we are, we can cease being players in a staged
game.

Secrets Men Keep
by Dr. Ken Druck

It is our prayer the people in our lives will know this book is not about blame. There is no intention to deal hurt.

Our lives are illustrations of the Hand of God weaving the dark threads with the light to make life beautiful. May this book help you discover His hand in your life.

Cindy and Wade Robinson

CHAPTER ONE
CHILDHOOD THROUGH HIGH SCHOOL
Cindy Robinson

My nickname was Sukey Blue Skin. My cousins gave me the name. I accepted it without understanding and didn't understand why until clear into my adulthood.

Like many pastors' kids, my young life is marked by where we lived. Here's what I mean:

At Litchfield, IL, my sister, Ethelyn, brother, Rob, and I had scarlet fever. We were quarantined three weeks, and Dad lived in the parlor.Mom slid meals to him through the front door. She had to disinfect all our dishes and clothes separately. All the shades had to be pulled to protect our eyes from damage.

My brother, Lowell, and I played our games here. We played what we called "Landing over." In this game, we jumped from the bed onto a chair.

I was about six when in one of the jumps, I landed on the knob of the chair rather than the seat. I screamed beyond belief, and to this day, I have a permanent dimple just where it belongs.

No one would guess I didn't come into the world with it. It's actually been fun to have in spite of the permanent knot on the inside of my cheek.

The house also had a separate garage where
Dad hung butchered hogs. W played "Handy
Over" at that garage. I must hve run around it a
zillion times.

I remember Litchfield's yard. About 1942, we
were playing outside until dusk, and typically kid-
like, didn't want to go in. Father called a couple of
times, but we did not respond. Suddenly this white,
ghost-like apparition sneaked into the yard and
scared us beyond belief. Once we calmed down,
we discovered our ghost was our father! We scur-
ried inside.

In 1945 I played with a 'Negro' – which was a
proper, respectful thing to say at that time in our
area, as Black or African-American is now – girl
named Donna. We were good friends. Old Brother
Ring, a minister friend had given me a Negro baby
doll.

Because of my friendship with Donna, he
knew I would appreciate it. I grew to love and
cherish the baby doll. When it came time to move,
Dad insisted I had to give the baby doll to Donna.
Through the years, I didn't think about the loss of
the baby too much.

The Litchfield kitchen is where my spiritual journey began. Kneeling at a kitchen chair, at
Mom's invitation, I first opened my heart to Jesus.

These were carefree days as I remember them.
I particularly remember Sunday afternoon walks

headed up by a man named Aaron Caulk. He "herded" his children and the parsonage children down the railroad tracks to out of the way places. He taught us about leaves, trees, and nature. We learned how to pick up hickory nuts and shell them.

I remember walking to the library, checking out books, reading them, and taking them back. The library was often the focus of life! Mother taught me that books are my friends. The love of books was instilled deep inside me, and continues with me today.

When we moved to Herrin, IL, my two brothers had to sleep on the back porch without heat or light. There was a drafty, old outhouse, equipped with the famous Sears catalog. A big dishpan served as a bathtub. A coal-burning stove kept one side of my body at a time warm during baths. Girls bathed after the boys – all quickly. There was no soaking in the tub or bubble bath in Herrin, IL.

I loved dolls and paper dolls. My favorite was a 'magic skin' doll. My father decided I needed to drink more milk, and promised me the magic skin doll I wanted if I'd drink its value in milk. I did, stoically! My Dad essentially paid double for the doll, even though the family's cash flow was not good at the time. It was a lousy way to get a doll. I hate milk.

Just at my sensitive young teen time of life (seventh grade), we moved into a house in rural Greenville, IL. It was two stories, uninviting, ugly and up on a hill.

My Dad's father, who had hardening of the arteries, lived alone in the house a few months before we moved in. In his demented state, he'd shot holes in the walls. He thought he was rescuing his small children, who in reality were grown men and women, from some unknown danger. When we first lived there, we stuffed rags in the bullet holes to keep out the winter's cold.

We carried water from an old well at the bottom of the hill. One time I what I thought was a cute baby mouse at the well. I went to the house to show Mother. She didnt' like my trophy and ordered me outside with it.

She firmly said, "Take that thing out of here!"

Outhouses, no heat in the shared bed rooms, steep, dark stairways, bricks wrapped in towels to keep feet warm at night and snow piles on the *inside* of the window sills are all part this house's memories.

Dad built a double garage, with the idea of us living in it while he tore down the old house and built a new one. My brother Rob liked to chin himself on the 2x4's to build up his muscles. But the time of living in the garage with unfinished walls and ceilings was to no avail. Dad was appointed to pastor a different church and he sold the land. Another old parsonage took the garage's place.

I was a sophomore in high school the year we moved into the Mt. Vernon house.

It had electricity! And an indoor bathroom!

Ethelyn was at Greenville College and Rob was already in the Navy. Lowell's back porch bedroom still didn't have any heat. He shared it with a new wringer washing machine!

When Ethelyn came home to visit, we still shared a room, but we had heat and electricity. It was the last house of my childhood.

Even my memories are less childlike.

I had a friend named Nancy, and we spent a lot of time at each other's houses. Like most young girls, we dreamed about romantic things and wanted to learn about love. Nobody ever talked to us about it.

We were reading the forbidden "True Story Magazine" at my house when Father caught us.

His intense anger startled me. Without considering the magazine belonged to Nancy, he grew so angry, he threw the magazine into the stove while I stood humiliated and speechless at his actions.

I remember a boy named Jim, a boy my parents didn't approve of, but I really liked. One awful saturday afternoon Dad took him and me on a ride aroudnt he fairground. Dad drove, I was in the front, and Jim was in the back.

Dad decreed I was not to see him anymore at church or school, and certainly not outside of any planned group activity! As Dad was driving, I was to tell Jim I could no longer see him. I did so verbally, but wrote him a note saying, "I'll see you at school." and wadded it up in my hand. While Dad was lowering the boom, I let it drop so Jim could see it. Delicious!

I didn't get caught that time, but later at camp meeting, my Dad caught me talking to him when I was wearing my housecoat. My Dad did not think I or the situation was cute. Again, I experienced his fierce anger.

I learned to drive while we lived at Mt. Vernon. This became one of my passions. I also landed my first part-time job during Christmas vacation at Woolworth's.

Woolworth's was what was known as a 'Dime Store, 'Variety Store', or 'Five and Dime Store.' They've been extinct for a while, with Wal-Mart and K-Mart taking their places.

Anyway, this job gave me some sense of self-esteem and confidence.

From MT. Vernon we took a trip as a family to Washington DC, Virginia and down through North Carolina.

I was growing up. But that increased the tenion between my Father and me. As I tested the boundaries, he grew more stern and more watchful of my actions. He was determined to keep me out of any trouble, which really translated to sexual involvement.

I don't miss any of the houses of my childhood, nor the places really. But the memories of early childhood are mostly pleasant. Some were even carefree; particularly the memories of Mother playing Fox Trots and Waltzes on our old upright piano.

Wednesday was often bread baking day for my mother. Fresh bread was a real treat for our friends and us after Wednesday evening service. But I also looked forward to Thursdays. On that day, Mother helped two young women do laundry (in Lowell's unheated bedroom), and they made yeast donuts.

I could smell them cooking when I turned the corner as I walked home from school. My pace got faster the closer to the house I got. Mother made enough for the neighbors, so often they gathered there, too.

I remember church camp meetings at Greenville Durley Camp and Cowden, IL. Like most Free Methodists my age, I remember the shouting, the children's services, flannelgraph Bible stories, the sawdust, the dining hall meals, and 5-cent bottles of soda pop.

Also, like most people my age, I remember ration stamps, outhouses, penny candy, and coal stoves. I also remember waiting for the ice truck that sold a block of ice for a quarter, and butchering days. Once a dog stole the hog out of the garage at Litchfield. Talk about activity! What a chase! Dad lost.

In Greenville, lightning struck the old house on a sunny, Saturday afternoon. Outside, where mother and my siblings were gathered, I could see their shock when I came out with soot covering my face and body. I had stubbed my toe on the way down the pitch dark, steep stairs and had fallen. My heart beat so hard, it felt like it was coming out of my chest.

Even at that age, I understood the magnitude of the cleaning up process. Everything had a layer of soot on it. But we were all safe, and we were grateful.

The highlight of my young years was several summer trips to Oklahoma to visit my maternal grandparents. My Father was from rural Wakita, and Mother was from near Oklahoma City. When she was five, her parents moved to rural Wakita, just four miles from where the Hunsakers lived.

We traveled 700 miles one-way on Route 66 in a 1935 Chevy pick-up truck. My father had built a canopy like thing over the bed to protect us from the hot Kansas and Oklahoma sun or their sudden rainstorms.

There were no conveniences such as truck stops, fast foods, or interstates.

We couldn't afford motels on the way. More often than not we stopped alongside a cornfield, pulled out cots and camped for the night.

There were no McDonalds so we stopped in small towns along Route 66 (there were no interstates either) for bologna, bread, milk - and sometimes chocolate milk and cookies.

We always stayed two weeks at Grandma's house. Those two weeks featured fish fries at Great Salt Lake Dam (near Jet) and watermelon feeds in Grandma's back yard.

The grade school across the narrow road from Grandma's was handy for me to play on the student's equipment. Those days school playgrounds were open, not fenced in and shut up during the summer.

I spent lots of time with Connie, a great cousin. We picked red current off the bushes. We played 'cook' in Grandma's underground cellar. We made gourmet mud pies in a miniature pie tin Grandma had. (I still have the pie tin and Connie and I are still friends.)

And, Grandma always had store bought candy! It was a special treat.

Summer church camps are the next to best memories of my childhood.

They were ten days then. Some summers we stayed in tents with straw ticks (a large gunnysack the size of a bed that was filled with straw and sewn together) until Dad built a rugged cabin with a tin roof over it.

I still cherish the memory of listening to the rain on that tin roof.

The other kids and I shared play, children's meetings, flannel graph stories and a general good time. But these also were the times I opened my sensitive heart and soaked up God's claim on my heart. And, in contrast to our parsonage environment, I felt more freedom to experience God's love for me.

For several years before I was nine, I'd vaguely been aware of my father's staunch rules. For instance, my name is Cynthia Florine. I was given the name Cynthia by Dad's college classmates at Greenville College in Greenville, IL. Florine came from my maternal grandmother. However, because a close friend of my mother *knew* a 'wicked' woman named Cynthia, they could not bear to call me Cynthia. So I was called by my middle name, Florine.

Anyway, when I was nine, my mother went to Oklahoma to be with her mother during a crisis there. She left my siblings and me with Dad for two weeks. I remember the emptiness of missing her. When I cried through a Sunday evening service, I was scolded. My father insisted I had nothing to cry about. The rules didn't allow pastors' little girls to cry during services.

The summer I was fourteen, a new boy moved near my Aunt's house. One Saturday I was in a hurry to go to town to see the new boy. However, my father would not go until he had combined (a combine is a harvesting machine) enough beans to make a truck load.

Between my father's insistence on waiting, my impatience, and our conflict of wills, I got to town, but not exactly like either of us planned.

In those days, ladies still ripped apart the colorfully designed cloth sacks cattle feed was shipped in, washed them, and made dresses out of them. I got ready for town, wearing one of these dresses with buttons down the front. Jeans for girls were forbidden. To hurry things along, I made my father a sandwich and took it and cookies to the field.

I approached the tractor and saw a handy ledge to step on to hoist myself onto the tractor. What I didn't know was the ledge was the combine's power take off. The next thing I knew I was on the ground, naked, bleeding, and shocked.

My father heard the motor miss rhythm and turned to witness my dress wrapped around the shaft. According to my father, if I'd had on jeans or a new dress of stiffer fabric, my body would have been "wrapped around the shaft."

The field was close to the road, and I had no clothes on. My father told me to get under the wagon to hide my nudity, went to the house, and told my mother to bring me clothes. Mother was shocked.

Then we went to town! Not to sell a load of beans. Not to see the cute new boy. But to get stitches in one eyebrow where a flying button caught me and a cast for my left ankle.

God and a dress saved my life.

However, as I began becoming my own person, the conflict with Dad's rules came into focus. They stifled my personality and any spark of creativity.

For years, I heard "Vanity, vanity, all is vanity" from my father. Sometimes he said it with a smile, but it always had a serious undertone. Along with that, he emphasized not thinking more highly of (myself) ourselves than (I) we ought. And somehow, that also meant what other people thought, because we were to always put everyone else before ourselves. He taught me modesty and "Be ye holy, for I am holy."

My self-talk became negative. "Don't think highly of yourself." I didn't even notice when the ***too highly*** became ***highly*** of yourself. "Vanity, all is vanity," covered anything my father didn't approve of. "Be Ye Holy"… and here are the rules to make you look and act holy.

I came to think of God as judgment bent, making sure I obeyed his rules to look holy, not a personal God whose goal was to change me so I could be holy.

My father *was* a godly man. But he only knew how to be the protector, self-appointed bodyguard he'd become when a car wreck took his mother when he was eighteen years old. His father had a 'nervous breakdown' and left my father with the family obligations of caring for a younger brother and sister.

My grandmother hadn't become a Christian until my Dad was a teenager. Dad and some of his siblings followed her example, and some did not. Dad always prayed for them. He longed to keep the family intact. He wanted his children to know their cousins.

My father did not have an example to help him learn nurturing of young spirits. He was well meaning in his legalistic, conservative, and God-fearing ways. Yet with his siblings, my mother, my siblings, and me, his need to control often overpowered the many good qualities in him.

In 1936, Dad took Mother with his two small children and traveled by train from Missouri to Greenville College in Greenville, IL. He felt God had called him to preach and he wanted a college education. Mother also had hopes of enrolling in college along with Dad.

However, I was the "oops" that destroyed her plans. It was a dark time for her. She re-adjusted her thinking and finally was able to welcome me to her world.

During her own childhood, she had developed an inferiority complex. Her habit had become to step back from control, and that made this transition more tolerable.

So Dad easily became the decision maker in the home.

About five years after she married, she was driving in the Ozarks in Missouri after dark and lost control of the car. She became very frightened and wouldn't drive at all after that.

This made her completely dependent upon Dad. She deferred to him and gradually allowed his ways to become all of her ways.

Yet, my mother was a fabulous homemaker. She was a peacemaker, a romantic and wanted everyone to love everyone. She had the gift of hospitality and entertained graciously in all the parsonages of Dad's ministry. I heard it may times, "Everyone loves Jewel."

Even though she was loved for herself, she chose not to buck Dad's controlling dominance. Through it all, she found her own 'comfort zone' in which to live and serve.

So, by the time I was fourteen, my main unconscious activity was seeking approval. I began to retreat on the inside. I split off and became three persons…. Not in the clinical sense, but in what part of myself I presented to the world.

To myself, I was an inferior, inadequate, insignificant person. I thought of myself as the "poor little Hunsaker girl" with no feelings, and no opinions.

To my small church group, I became the leader of the pack. I organized the youth groups, sang special songs, and gave testimonies.

At school, I was a little mouse in a corner. I was quiet and unassuming. I never wanted to draw attention to myself for fear someone would notice I was different. I hated being called on in class. Even if I knew the right answer, I couldn't confidently give it.

At the same time, I became the consummate preacher's kid – a peacemaker and example. But I always felt guilt, as I never quite lived up to the standards held up for me. I struggled to live up to the name my mother gave me as she overcame her disappointment of my untimely arrival; her 'Ray of Sunshine." Yet, I desperately wanted to be like my invincible, religious father.

All this unexpressed, underlying tension took its toll. My junior year in high school, I was too ill to attend a full day of school, and attended half days.

I rested every afternoon, according to doctor's orders. I read a lot of books and wrote letters to "Pen Pals." And I read the Bible every day, trying to be spiritual.

The doctor said it was anemia. Fifty years later, I learned it was the origin of the nickname my cousins gave me. To them, Sukey Blue Skin described the color of my pale skin.

I was too ill to attend high school graduation. I had a very bad 'spring cold,' and was enduring Dad's old fashioned remedy: the classic steaming water in a teakettle, towel tent over my head, and inhalation of 'Vicks' while breathing in the steam. I hated it. I vowed to never do that when I grew up!

Part of me felt sad I wasn't part of the graduation as it accentuated my feelings of being an outsider. Yet, part of me was relieved I didn't have to go. I was a member of a large, several-hundred student class. I couldn't face the bustle of activities, not feel a part of them, and face my own internal torment over what I saw as inadequacies.

So I was home, stuffed up with a cold while the

rest of the class graduated, and the new graduation dress my sister had taken my mother and I to
buy a couple of weeks earlier hung in my closet.
Ethelyn did take a picture of me in the dress, and
one of me in my cap and gown that I'd already
picked up.

I dont' remember any great show of emotions
about it. Nor do I remember any expressions of
sorrow for comfort, or encouragement for help.

In hindsight, I know the illness was a cop-
out. An escape from the tension, my own sense
of inadequacies,and insecurities.

CHAPTER TWO

MIXED BLESSINGS.... REFLECTIONS
CINDY ROBINSON

In spite of everything, some important things came out of those years.

After the first trauma of crying in the first grade and my teacher calling my big brother out of his class to take me home, I did like school. I loved English, hated math. I loved winning spelling bees.

And I did have some close friends. At Herrin, from ages nine through eleven, my best friend was Rosalie. She was at my house more than I was at hers, as we had more material comforts than her family. Rosalie's sister was also my sister's best friend. (And I had a childhood crush on her brother.)

The thing I remember most about her family had to do with the expression of their emotions. Rosalie's family celebrated Memorial Day. Ours did not. They went to a town more than an hour away just to decorate graves. Then they went on a family outing. Mostly they went the fair, and I often got to go with them. I'll never forget the honeysuckles and other vines they used to decorate the graves and the rides at the fair.

Elliott was my first real interest in boys. I was a freshman at Greenville High School. We walked to weekly band concerts at the town square in the summer. Sometimes, he would meet me at the school gym for ball games. This didn't happen often because Father did not allow me to go to town very often. I don't remember any close girl friends from Greenville. In truth, my closest friends were my cousins (the ones who gave me *the* nickname).

The only thing I learned about the male-female relationship from my parents was you didn't talk about love and/or sex. They seemed taboo. That word wasn't used, but we knew. Mother insisted if I kissed a guy, it was as binding as if we were engaged! Sitting on a boy's lap was pure sin... the worst. Still when, at fifteen, I fell Jim (the one my parents didn't approve of) they found me a substitute.

Jim wasn't a churchgoer. He drank. Dad considered him 'wild.' I think that was the attraction, along with him being three years older than I was. Jim did start to church and professed to quit smoking. But all that was over quick when Dad caught me sneaking out to meet him.

My parents 'encouraged' me to 'like' Dick, a boy from a good Free Methodist family in a town ninety miles away. I'd known him from camp meetings since I was nine. This was a long distance, letter-writing relationship.

We learned to travel the C&EI Railway to visit one another. After a short bevy of letter writing and parent approved visits, Dick wrote me a Dear John letter. He'd found a girlfriend closer to home. And that was that. I was still just sixteen. My navy brother wrote me a letter of comfort and encouragement.

Strangely enough, I really wanted a lifetime marriage. I wanted to be a great cook, a good hostess, and preside over an open house like my mother. I wanted people to 'love Florine' like 'everyone loves Jewel'. I don't know if I even equated a relationship with a man with these activities.

My desire to be like my father seems strange to me now. I had no real emotional connection with him, yet I admired his missionary mindedness, and his spiritual strength. He went on five missionary trips himself.

When he had an evangelist lay hands on me and pray for me to be a missionary, he was trying to pass that on to me.

Dad did not neglect raising us to know about God. He instilled in me a love of the Scripture and taught me Christian values. Even when we were in full conflict of wills, for there was no room for individual expression in Dad's view of things, I still wanted to be like him.

I didn't understand many of the things my father insisted we do. If I had understood them as a child it may have driven me to be more like him. Or I may have realized like my brother, Lowell, seemed to, many of the rules came from Dad and not God's word.

In 1997, unknown to me, Lowell, told our eighty-nine year old Dad he (Dad) needed to make amends with me for insisting I give up my precious doll.

I suppose Dad had also come to realize much of what that generation of ministers and fathers did was about control, and not God. So Dad built a wooden doll cradle, using some deep blue Plexiglas from his VISA (Volunteer missionary organization of our denomination) trip to Haiti for decoration.

My Dad paid for the black doll of my siblings choosing. Mother made miniature pillows and a coverlet. Lowell's wife, Janet, crocheted a tiny afghan. In February 1998, Dad presented his "'I'm sorry" gift to me. We laughed and cried as we talked about my "Negro" dolly of fifty-three years earlier.

Because of the control thing, I spent a lot of time at altars. I never measured up to the view of God my Dad gave me. And every strong preacher at camp or revival sent me to the altar, seeking relief from the guilt. Often I didn't know if my relationship with God was intact because of the guilt. For the next forty years, I was haunted by this God of judgment, and legalism.

Yet, that precious gift of loving God is the most important gift from childhood that survived. Since age five, when I knelt with my mother, I've wanted only to serve God. And that has never left me. For that, I am grateful.

Camp meeting is part of that heritage. It's a time set aside to focus on spiritual things and fellowship with others. It gave me time away from a disapproving father being my dominant focus. I had friends. I felt part of the whole of thing. My three personas became one while I was at camp. And that was part of my childhood gift.

I knew, somehow, God was the answer. Even if not much else positive can be said about my childhood, this was a great gift.

Another gift came from my mother. Although we weren't close, nor was she able to counteract my father's domination, she gave me encouragement and an example. Although she never quite felt adequate for the job, and felt apologetic for her efforts, she became the model pastor's wife. Her house was always filled with the comforting smells of cooking and cleanliness. And she could make that old piano rock!

She and Dad took in a family to stay a few days - but became weeks.

Dad's sister, Thelma, was already was living with us.

Before the family arrived, my sister and my aunt – in one single act of rebellion - took down their favorite curtains from the bedroom they had to abandon to the new family. Dad didn't appreciate that at ALL, and made them put the curtains back up.

Maybe the weeks became months—I don't remember. Mother never said a word, and remained quietly stable through it all. She even remained calm when we discovered we had to decontaminate the house because when they left, they left us their bedbugs!

Another time Mother became so frightened by something she read in the paper that she put on a headscarf and sweater, turned off the lights, and hid behind the door with a coal poker until the rest of the family returned from a ball game. She was glad it was her family who came through the door! We were glad she didn't use the coal poker!

She defended Dad's decision to make me wear long, brown stockings to school. She told me to tell my girl friends, "If you had a thimble full of sense, you would wear them too," when I complained I would be laughed at. I was laughed at, but refused to pass on mother's sage advice.

But again, mother laughed and seemed carefree when a lady named Waldine attended camp
meeting with us. Their laughing was far noisier
than any of us kid's commotion. I could never
figure out what adults could find so funny, but it
was good to hear my mother laugh.

One time mother panicked and called in the
neighbors to look for me when I'd, unknown to
her, returned to the house after being outside. I
went to the boys' room and went to sleep. I don't
remember the conversation we had when she realized I was safe.

She became the surrogate mother to a family
of kids when their mother died as well as to a
newly divorced young woman with several small
children... and who knows how many others.
It's interesting to me that the kids of these two
families became close friends through the years.
The divorced young woman became like another
daughter.

Mother's always been a romantic – wanting
everyone to find the right person to love. She
stuck with Dad in his decision: I was to give
the boy of his choice a chance even though he
dumped me two years earlier. I was too naive to
realize this didn't show me any consideration or
respect of my own choices. Hindsight makes me

realize Dad was concerned about me going in the right direction in life, and certainly not to get into any sexual involvements.

Needless to say, my childhood left me struggling with conflicts about my own sexuality, male-female relationships, God, religion, and my own value. Who was I? What did I believe about anything? I had very little voice to speak up for myself.

My father's ambition for my life's work as a missionary left me wondering what I was to be, as I didn't share it. I felt I hadn't lived up to his expectations of me.

I had no real experience on making independent decisions. Unprepared, I blindly accepted my parents' plan for my future. Yet, God was at work, molding, shaping, and preparing me for His service.

I didn't know that yet, so I took confusion, inferiority, and a deep longing to serve God with me to college.

CHAPTER THREE

EARLY YEARS TO HIGH SCHOOL
WADE ROBINSON

So, I want to tell you the way it was growing up in Winnsboro, Louisiana.

I was named after my paternal grandfather, Mansford Wade Robinson, who I never knew. He was deceased before I was born. But I was always told he was a strong person with a tender heart.

He owned several hundred acres of cotton land. My father grew up on that land, and so did my brother, two sisters, and I.

My Daddy was a good man. He had a stick–to–it ability. He was strong, tall, and determined. But in his early years, before he was married, he had typhoid fever. A doctor, who was a distant cousin of my father's, treated him for everything but Typhoid – quinine for malaria mostly. Finally, another doctor was called in. He took one look at Daddy.

"This man has typhoid fever!" And treatment for that was begun.

But it was too late. The high fever had already affected his brain. He had trouble thinking, making decisions, and using good judgment. He related to life and other people more like a child than an adult.

I grew up from birth to college on the same property and lived in two houses, not very far from each other. The second at least had running water. By then I was the only child left. But I remember the first house on the farm best.

It was an old house that just had boards on the outside, and was unfinished on the inside. All the two-by-fours in the structure were exposed.

The floor was made of boards also, and they didn't fit together real good. In fact, there were times I could watch the chickens run around under the house.

I could see the smoke as it drifted from the chimney.

When it snowed, the flakes would come drifting through the boards. Now, when it rained, it would not come in, but when it snowed, the wind could blow the snow right in.

The house had three rooms. The living room doubled as my parents' bedroom. Of course, we had a kitchen. And the third room was us kids' room. It had two beds. The girls shared one, and we boys shared the other.

It was cold in the wintertime. We heated the house with an old fireplace. We'd have to keep turning around and around to keep warm on all sides. And yes, Saturday night baths were taken in the old washtub in water heated on the stove.

My first real sharp memories begin at around age two. I had, or what they called at the time, colitis. They took me to the doctor who put me in what they called the clinic.

I was very near death. My father finally left the room to keep from watching me die. Imagine his surprise when I revived.

"Your eyes had set in your head like a dead person's," he explained, telling me why he was certain I was going to die.

I spent my second birthday in the clinic. And when I got out, I had a long road to recovery. I had to watch carefully what I ate. Certain foods I had to avoid and only a few things was I allowed to eat.

In that weakened condition, I caught every flu bug that flew by and every cold whose germs floated in my area. Even after I went to school, I continued to be "sickly"- as was the expression of the day.

Going to school is another story. Picture a six year old walking a mile in the wintertime when the frost covered the ground – the ground was sometimes frozen – and waiting before daylight for the bus to show up. Actually, I rode two busses to get to and from school.

The first bus was an old truck with wooden benches in it, with a tarp thrown over it the top. We'd ride that bus two miles over dirt roads.

Then we'd switch to the second bus and ride into town. After school, we had to wait an hour while the bus that took us out of town made another run. Then it took us to the dirt road, where we waited for the truck with the benches and tarp. In the winter it was sometime after dark by the time I got home.

My grade school memories are mixed. They vary from very good to tragic.

I remember catching white-faced bumblebees and tying them on a string. I let them fly around, but only where I went, holding the string.

My playmates were mostly my cousins who lived nearby. I made a stick horse and went wherever I wanted to go.

I built a four foot long by two-foot wide car that sat in one place. I built the steering wheel, brakes, clutch, and other parts of the car out of blocks, boards, sticks and whatever I could find. I reckon I traveled 20,000 miles or more in that car.

I hunted rats, birds and snakes with a BB gun my brother helped me get when I was seven.

I liked to roll buggy tires – 20,000 miles or so.

I had a dog named Trixie. Dad had cows, a horse, chickens, and a hog to butcher.

I remember with distaste picking cotton. In the fall, which is cotton picking time. I'd get home from school, have a piece of bread – maybe with some jelly on it – and a glass of water. Then, I'd get my cotton sack. And I picked cotton. When I would look up and consider the acreage, I got discouraged.

"I'll never get it done," I'd think. I got through it by concentrating on one row at a time. "I'll get through this row," I'd asure myself. And I did.

Overriding the good times was illness, hunger, and feelings of inferiority.

My older brother helped me get a bicycle that broadened my life. But I'd wanted one since I was eight or nine. At Christmas time Mother used to take five dollars and to town to buy something for her four children.

Now, I'd always been told to be good and Santa would bring gifts. I was really good the year I was nine (or eight). Christmas morning, I looked for a bike.

It wasn't under the tree, so I went outside and looked. It was not there.

Mother came out and was truthful. "Wade, there is no Santa Clause. You've been really good this year, but I didn't have the money to get you the bike you wanted."

Reality and disappointment crashed in together.

About this time, a female cousin of mine was standing in front of an open fireplace when her clothes caught on fire. She lived for three months, and my mother spent a lot of time the hospital in New Orleans helping out. I missed Mother.

My teacher asked for updates on my cousin's condition from time to time. One day I told the class she quit breathing and was revived.

"There is no such thing," my teacher scoffed.

She embarrassed me thoroughly, even though it was true. On top of me being upset about my cousin, my self-esteem took another nosedive.

When I was twelve, my brother-in-law's mother was dying. She moaned and groaned all day. I felt relief when she died.

When I was thirteen, a fifteen-year-old friend drowned. An uncle of mine died that year. And, when I was fourteen, my grandmother Netherland died.

I began to realize I too would pass that mile soon. I became afraid of death.

School itself followed the same pattern. There were good things about it and some bad things.

In the first grade, I dropped a snack my mother sent with me on the bus and an older kid stepped on it accidentally. The bus driver saw what happened and my tears. He gave me some coins to buy a cinnamon roll from a nearby bakery. When my sister and I went to the bakery, we discovered we had enough money for both of us. So, I had a friend looking out for me.

I'm afraid I did cry at school during my first year. I tried to do it in private, but when my class-mates saw me and told my teacher, I could not tell her I cried because I missed Mother.

I would not be laughed at.

My second grade teacher kept me back a year because of a misunderstanding. At the end of the year, she went down the rows, telling each kid "You pass," or "You didn't pass." I was so ner-vous about the whole thing, and afraid I wouldn't pass, when she came to me, I looked up at her tearfully.

"If I didn't pass, can I stay in your room next year?" I asked.

She assumed I meant I wanted to stay in her room another year and didn't tell me I passed.

On the whole, I liked my teachers except the fifth grade teacher. For some reason, she liked to embarrass me in front of the class. Her ridicule heightened my sensitivity and chipped away at my self-esteem.

By the time I was going into the fifth grade, the doctors began to suspect something was wrong with my heart. There *was* something wrong with me but what it was, we did not know. I was always sick and ran a fever a lot.

The doctor told me I had an enlarged heart. That scared the "doo-do" out of me and for years, I was afraid to go to sleep at night for fear I would die.

I was told not to do anything that would make me tired. He wrote and excuse for me to stay out of school a whole year. And that year I did not go to school for one day. That put me really behind all the rest of the students.

One thing this year did was foster my love for hunting. I've always wanted to hunt. One of my passtimes during that year was noning my hunting skills with birds as the targets. I quickly graduated from a slingshot to a BB gun. I can still remember the day Daddy was gone and a bevy of blackbirds gathered in our yard. Mother let me use the double barrel 12-guage shotgun with eared hammers and I killed several of the birds.

Let me tell you, the old double barrel "kicked this little fella'" pretty hard.

I graduated to rabbits and squirrels. There were no deer in that area, so I didn't hunt deer until I was in High School.

And, by the time I was a teenager in high school, I had developed quite an inferiority complex. My clothes were hand-me-downs, or made by my mother out of flour sacks. My shoes tore up. Once I took a piece of cloth and glued it inside my tennis shoe to make it last longer. Well, of course, the glue didn't last long and soon the piece of cloth was sticking out.

But that's all I had, so I just wore them.

We didn't have a car, so as soon as I was old enough, I hitch hiked into town and other places I wanted to go.

Between my junior and senior years in high school, several things happened. I hitch hiked to Monroe, LA and stayed with my brother there.

Through some friends from back home who were there, I met a girl named Vera.

Now, I really don't remember a time when I wasn't interested in girls. (My mother was really upset when she learned I had learned where babies came from when I was eleven.) But Vera was my first serious girlfriend.

Vera and I went out a few months, and soon were engaged.

At the same time, one spiritual journey was coming to an end and another was beginning. As early as six, I wanted to go forward in the church we attended.

"No, Wade, you are much too young. You do not know what you are doing," my Mother counseled, and held me back.

I did not give my heart to God at that time.

But at age seventeen, I'd gone to a church where they had a lot of emotions and they spoke in tongues and beat their drums and stomped their feet. One time, the preacher there had given an invitation, and I was willing to get up and go forward and ask God into my heart.

But a sweet spirit came by and said to me, "Wade, this is not what you are looking for."

Sometime between my junior and senior years, I went to a revival in Columbia and listened to a man named Arthur Roney preach. He was a Free Methodist evangelist, and he presented the gospel in such a way I recognized it.

That sweet spirit came by and said, "Wade, this is what you are looking for."

Because of my previous experience, I thought I had to struggle and pray loud and long. The conversation in my head was between the sweet spirit and another voice.

"This is indeed what you are looking for."

"You'll have to quit the picture shows, the skating, the swimming, and you'll never have any fun."

"But this is what you want."

Although I made a lot of progress that night, I was exhausted from the struggle. I really did not get to know Jesus.

But the strong desire to know Jesus that had been in me since I was six did not go away.

That summer… it must have been June because it was cotton hoeing time… that same evangelist was holding a revival in my sister's home church.

I wanted to go. But there was a lot of grass in the cotton that needed to be hoed out. I approached my parents – my Mother actually, as she made the family decisions.

"Wade," she said. "We need to hoe this cotton."

"Yes, Ma'am, I know it needs to be hoed. But I want to go to the revival. I want to be saved."

"Well, Wade, you're already a good boy."

"Yes, but I need to be saved. If you let me get saved, I'll come back and do the work."

Mother gave in. "I guess it will be all right."

So, I took a few clothes and put them in a bag. I hitch hiked to a friend's house in another town. And we went together to yet another small town to my sister's home church.

Now, I have no idea what the preacher preached about. My thoughts were churning.

"Why does he have to preach so long? Why can't he just give the invitation so I can go forward?"

Finally, it was time to give the invitation, and I was the first to go forward.

I knelt there a couple of minutes and I gave my heart to God. I didn't feel any emotion. I didn't feel any different from what I had felt before church. I just didn't have any feelings whatsoever. No bells rang, no thunder sounded, no lights flashed before me.

But I knew I was sorry for my sins. I knew I'd asked Jesus to come in. And I knew He came in and He'd saved me. He promised He would, and I believed it.

I knelt there just a few minutes more, went back, and sat down.

Vera and I were engaged before I came to know Jesus and gave my heart to Him. She was not living a Christian life, and God began dealing with me about that. I knew the Bible said "Be ye not unequally yoked together." But I was in love.

She was my first girlfriend. Shouldn't I love her?

And yet, I was torn in two different directions.

God said, "Will you give her up?"

My desire was to keep her.

I remember sitting in high school class that fall and listening to the argument in my head.

"Are you going God's way or your way? Are you going to tell her good-bye, or continue with her?"

And I sat there in class looking out the window. I don't know how long I sat there, but finally I heard the teacher, who was the wife of a distant relative.

"Wade! You are not doing your work."

I couldn't tell her what was on my mind, but I knew I'd have to settle it. I didn't know what to do.

One day, not long after that, I got a letter from Vera. Well, really, it was a Dear John letter. I took that letter and walked down in the woods.

There was this little scoop of woods past my parents' house, and that's where I went. I knelt down in a little ditch kind of thing and prayed.

"God, I give this to you. I give this girl up. I surrender this decision to you. And I ask you to make all the decisions from now on. Have your way in my life." And I remember the peace that came over my life.

Vera later repented of writing the letter, saying she didn't know why she wrote it. She wanted me to take her back. She even came to the school house and asked me to go riding with her, and wanted me to come back and be her boyfriend again. But I had to tell her no.

As I got closer to God, Mother began to have a closer walk with the Lord. I took the lead, and began having nightly devotions with my parents.

I remember becoming aware of my Dad's meal prayer. I don't know how long I'd heard it three times a day. "Gracious Lord, give us thankful heart for these table comforts which we are about to receive. Forgive our sins and save our souls in Christ's name. Amen."

"Daddy," I said. "Haven't we already asked Him to forgive our sins? We don't need to do that every time we pray."

Dad agreed, and began being more creative in his praying. All three of us began attending the Winnsboro Free Methodist Church. Someone would come to the house every Sunday, take us to church, and see that we got home.

In March of 1955, my pastor was holding a meeting at a little church near Jonesville, LA. That Friday when school was out, I drove my pastor's car that he'd left for his wife to use, and drove his wife and three kids to Oak Grove Free Methodist Church.

When we got there, the car had a flat tire. As I changed it, six or seven teenage girls walked up to talk to me. They initiated the conversation – talking to this new guy.

I'd never seen them before. I'd never been to Oak Grove church before. But they were very friendly. I remember the spokesperson. Her name was Ellen Luttrull.

After our first encounter, I didn't attempt to talk to them anymore that night.

But it planted a new thought in my head. "I'm without a girlfriend, and I'll be glad when I can find a Christian girlfriend."

Through the last months of my senior year, I had trouble trying to get all my school work done, with so little time allotted to me for study. By that time, I'd taken on more family responsibilities. I would pay the bills while I was in town, or go to the grocery store and buy what groceries I could carry in my hands on the bus. I was nearly overwhelmed a lot of the time.

When I looked at the yearbook, I saw where nearly all the students had something under their pictures and names: what clubs they belonged to, played football, played basketball, or played in the band. When it came to my picture, there was just "Wade Robinson." But I graduated. I'd reached a goal.

That summer there was a camp meeting in Louisiana Free Methodist Camp in Summerville, LA. It was my first time going to camp.

"Maybe I can find a Christian girlfriend there," I thought. I knew there just had to be several Christian girls there.

Now, we had a specific way of paying for meals at camp. We'd buy a meal ticket, and they'd punch your ticket to show you'd eaten. And you had to have a meal ticket before you could eat.

At one point, I was sitting at the same table with the girls from the church where I'd changed the flat tire. And it was the same girls. There they were. Some of them had gone forward and been saved at camp.

I was sitting at the end of the table where the person came to punch the tickets. The girls all passed their tickets up to me so the person could put the holes in them. I was not quite as dumb as some people gave me credit. I took those tickets and stuffed them into my pocket.

My reasoning was this: "If I take these tickets, they have to talk to me before they can get their tickets back." And eventually, they all came by and asked for their tickets.

All except Ellen Fay Luttrull. She knew I had it, but it didn't bother her. So, I kept her ticket the rest of the camp. We ate together. We sat in church together. We started a courtship.

When I was eighteen, my parents bought a 1936 Chevy truck for $135.00. I was the driver since neither of my parents drove a vehicle. I didn't have to walk, hitch hike, or depend on other people.

The pickup gave me some freedom, but it also added another dimension of ridicule from the kids.

It was a wonderful mess. The windows were missing, so I put tin in the open space to keep the wind out. The fenders were split, so I put metal strips on and bolted them together so they wouldn't break into two pieces. A leather strap fastened the driver's door shut. And a stick with a fork in it, balanced against the dash and the gearshift, kept it from popping out of third gear. It was in dire need of a paint job. I attached a piece of wood with the words "Always Late" written on it to the back of the truck.

Needless to say, my self-esteem took a beating. But I had a Christian girlfriend and wheels!

I was becoming an adult. I was glad to get out of my teens and into adulthood. I have never wanted to go back to them.

CHAPTER FOUR

REFLECTIONS OF CHILDHOOD
WADE ROBINSON

By grace you are saved through faith and that not of yourselves. It is a gift of God, not of works, lest any should boast. Ephesians 2:8-9

I've wondered about my fifteen year-old mother who married a man fifteen years older than she, and who was not quite normal. She had to make the family decisions, take care of finances, pay the bills, and be our source of discipline.

She was a remarkable woman. She was sweet, with a great sense of humor and she knew how to show affection. To me she didn't seem to be afraid of anyone. I remember her conversations with people in doctors' offices and about any other place we went.

I suppose the stillborn child she'd delivered just before she got pregnant with me made her extra protective of me. Of course, my general health contributed to that. On top of that, I was the youngest of the family … well, they all pampered me.

But the thing that haunted my childhood was the poverty. They say Daddy used poor judgment in how close he plowed to the cotton plants and stunted their growth. As a result, the plants didn't produce what it could have. So our income was even below other poor cotton farmers'. Often it wasn't even enough to cover basic needs of the family.

I was a sad, lonely kid because I was hungry a lot of the time. But the terrible inferiority complex, I think, was born not only of the poverty, it also had to do with the way my Daddy was. I didn't despise him, nor was I ashamed. But he wasn't like other fathers. I was very self-conscious about these two things.

I hated being poor. I despised picking cotton. Two resolves came from this complex I developed that have served me well.

The first resolve was "I will get through this." By concentrating on one row of cotton at a time, I resolved to get through cotton picking and hoeing. And I did.

The second was "I will get an education." I was not going to be a cotton farmer!

In those formative years, my Grandmothers played a stronger part in my life than I realized at the time.On the way home from the second bus ride of my school years, I passed my Grandmother Robinson's house. She usually had a snack of cornbread or a cookie for me. She read the Bible to me and prayed.

My Grandmother Netherland taught me some solid values:

Don't work on Sunday.

Be honest.

Don't take what belongs to someone else.

"Take anything anyone gives you," Grandmother would say. "Except a beating or a cussing."

I'm thankful for their influences.

There are two seemingly contradictory feelings I don't remember being without. As I have said, the first was interest in the opposite sex. The second was a longing to know Jesus. I reckon without the second, the first would have gotten me in a lot more trouble than it did.

I remember the first two pastor/evangelists who awakened the desire to know Jesus in me. I remember them well because of their names. Tom Ratcliff and Pastor A.C. Trap. Rat and Trap.

I suppose one of them was preaching in a "protracted meeting" on that hot, sultry summer afternoon my mother's good intentions checked my first desire to formally give myself to God.

Isaiah 42:3 says: "A bruised reed he will not break, and the smoking flax he will not quench." The desire smoldered on in spite of all efforts to smother it.

In the Methodist tradition of teaching theology through hymns and songs, I learned a song that went approximately like: "There's an all–seeing eye watching you, watching you, watching everything that you do."

As we stood around the kerosene lamps among the many flying insects at outdoor community meetings that were held in people's yards and sang that song, my imagination reached up to envision an eyeball somewhere in the sky as big as ten acres of cotton! God had to have an eye that big to see the whole world at once. But to me it wasn't oppressive. It was comforting.

Well, long ago, I dropped the big eyeball idea, but I still like the concept of God as being one who sees all and knows all.

I also came to know God was good to allow me to become a Christian like He did. I believe God could have given me some kind of passing emotional feeling that would have deceived me into believing I was saved without really putting my faith in Jesus. Had that been the case, when the feelings left, so would have my salvation. My feelings were always up and down. But God, in His tender patience helped me find that right path of faith in Jesus.

The feelings did come.

I was working in the cotton fields. "God," I prayed. "I know I'm saved, but it sure would be nice to have some feelings."

God honored that prayer with that wonderful assurance, and I "felt saved." Another great thing happened when I "felt saved." I lost my morbid fear of death.

When I took Vera's letter to the woods, and surrendered that struggle to God, I didn't know what to call the resulting feelings. I had testified to what some denominations call sanctification. Others call it a second work of grace, a deeper walk, complete submission, a higher walk, or being filled with the Holy Spirit.

Anyway, I'd professed it as I had grown in my faith, but I don't think the real work was done until I reached this place.

The main issue that got settled that day was not just "Would I quit seeing this girl?" It was "Would I let the Holy Spirit have my whole life? Would I let God end the rebellion inside of me?"

The end of this struggle to let God make my decisions and meeting Ellen went forward with me from childhood to adulthood.

I never looked back.

CHAPTER FIVE

COLLEGE THROUGH MARRIAGE
CINDY ROBINSON

The summer before I left for Greenville College I closed the childhood and teen years' chapters of my life with three major events, of course all planned by my dad.

First, my dad took a month of leave from his pastoral duties at the church he served that year. He took mother, my younger brother and myself on an extended trip to see our maternal grandparents and stayed with them two weeks. Then we went to Washington D.C. and visited all the historical places in that area, including the Washington Monument, and Washington's home. Finally we ended the trip in North Carolina, Camp Leguene, visiting my brother and his wife. Their first born had just entered the world and, of course, my mother needed to see her new granddaughter. I was delighted to see my first niece.

I found out many years later the trip wasn[t just for fun and vacation. Unknown to me, Dad had a reason for declaring that month long vacation.

Here's the story: For nearly a year, Dad had helped the Clevelands across the road from the church in a lot of ways. He provided rides to doctors, sometimes even paid for groceries and medicines. The man's son, Jim, was a drifter, but did come to church. Although he was fifteen years older than I was, he took a liking to me and sought my attention. Without me knowing it, Dad put a stop to his growing attentions by talking to Jim.

Evidently Dad believed Jim's threat to fix it so no one would want me if he wasn't allowed to take me out.

I didn't know the entire story until many years later, when I learned Dad did without his pay for that month, as the church had to have a preacher, and the fill-in got Dad's salary.

But Dad's purpose was accomplished. I barely had time to pack my bags for Greenville by the time we returned home. Jim sent me a dozen yellow roses after I'd been at college for three weeks, and then left me alone.

Secondly, this was the first summer I only attended Cowden Camp one day. That same day Dick and his family were visiting from Rochester, New York, where they lived at the time. Dick asked if I would write to him. I let him know I answer mail. Three days later, I got a letter. Once again, we began corresponding.

Although the encounter opened a closed relationship, I went off to Greenville College and he went to Roberts Wesleyan in Rochester, NY.

Going off to college was the third main event of the summer, and I went without educational goals or ambition.

I partially fulfilled my father's ambition for his children to attend his beloved Greenville. I was shy, afraid – a wallflower. I had no sense of value. I knew God loved me, but to people, I felt useless. I was lost, lonely, and frightened.

The kids around me must have seen something I didn't, as I did have friends, and began seeing a boy named Larry. We went steady for several months. We enjoyed being together. He believed in me. He encouraged me to do things, and I joined the Missions Club and Girls Glee Club.

I also met a boy named Wade Robinson. I had a class or two with him. However, he was engaged to a girl named Ellen at home in Louisiana. We were merely classmates.

During my freshman year, Dick's letters began begging me to come to New York where he lived at home while attending college, I really didn't want to go. But I didn't know how to say no. I consulted my mentor, and together we composed a firm 'no' letter.

Wanting to please my parents, very naively, I showed it to my parents. Quickly Dad said firmly, "Sis, you can't send a letter like that."

So, I didn't.

I broke up with Larry and went to New York because my parents approved and Dick was persistent. I lacked the ability to make my own decision.

My sophomore year at Roberts Wesleyan was unremarkable except one encounter. In Human Relations, we wrote papers as routine assignments. One day the professor asked me to stay after class.

"I'd like you to re-consider your engagement to Dick," he started, to my surprise. "You're both fine Christian young people," he continued. "I've known the family for years. They are a nice family, but the two of you and his family are not compatible."

Almost as if Dick knew my doubts, he initiated more and more intimate physical contact. He had always been 'handsey' (as we used to say) – even in our earlier relationship. I had never told my parents about that part of Dick's insistence. I was taught any intimate contact before marriage was a sin. Dick, on the other hand, insisted anything but sex was okay before marriage.

Physical contact was his answer to all issues we had. This threw me into terrible inner conflict with all my parents' set of moral values they had instilled in me.

And we disagreed and fought about nearly all issues.

I felt trapped. I was in unfamiliar territory, had no close relationships, felt inadequate, inferior, and confused.

My confusion became worse as I encountered an entirely different way of life in Dick's world. At home, we went to church a minimum of three occasions a week. They went on Sunday mornings. They ate out on Sunday, went to movies, wore jewelry, and lots of other things I was taught was 'sinful'.

And Dick's mother was a domineering woman who, I felt, didn't like me.

In spite of that I quit college, got a job as a nurses' aide, and then moved to floor secretary at Highland Hospital in Rochester, NY.

I worked for a year before, on June 7, 1958, I married Dick.

The wedding day wasn't happy as my domineering father and domineering mother-in-law-to-be clashed over pictures during the ceremony and rings. We had neither.

After the ceremony, we returned to North Chili, NY for Dick to finish his last year in college.

Sometime in the first two months of our brand new marriage, Dick decided to confess a sexual indiscretion in the months prior to my arrival in New York, but after we were "promised" to each other. In those days, "Promised" to each other meant something deeper than it does today.

"Why didn't you tell me before we were married?" I managed to ask.

"I didn't think you would marry me if you knew," was his defense.

We had some good times. Sunday afternoons were for rides in the car and long, philosophical talks with my father-in-law. We visited Niagara Falls. And we had our first child.

Kenneth Ray was born December 11, 1959. He was three weeks late. My doctor let me labor thirty hours because of my insistence for as natural a birth as possible. Ken's head began to become shaped like a cone, and we were both in trouble. The doctor went as far as to ask Dick which he would choose if only one of us could survive. While the family pondered, the doctor did a c-section. Dick didn't have to decide. Ken and I both lived. The nurses worked with re-shaping Ken's head so, when I saw him ten hours later, his head was perfect.

I put little nagging fears away. I was on my way to emulating my mother.

In January 1960, we moved to Shelbyville, IL, my husband's hometown. In September Dick had a job teaching school. But from January to September, we had no income. Dick made a little by fixing televisions now and then. His parents helped a lot. We even lived on the family's farm for about three months until his parents moved back from New York.

Dick's job finally started, and after a year in a rented house, we bought and remodeled an old house. My father-in-law did the majority of the work, and I was his helper. Sometimes I had varnish dripping off my elbows! I hated cleaning brushes!

We had a double garage, and lots of space for entertaining. And we did a lot of it. Extended family came for holidays. Many people came for many different occasions, especially his students.

But I was slowly becoming aware of a growing anger inside. I, having been raised with corporal punishment, used it with my children.

When Ken was about six, our dryer was next to the sink and we stacked dirty dishes on it.

As it happens in busy households, I automatically started the dryer without thinking about the consequences. Ken was in the kitchen while I went off to do something else. The crash of dishes as they jiggled off the vibrating dryer brought me running. I found Ken cowered in a corner. He assumed I would blame him. The look he gave me made me realize he was afraid of what I would do it him.

Instead of punishing him, I sat beside him and laughed at the mess. But the momentary fear in his eyes woke me up to my own harshness and forever changed the strength with which I disciplined my children.

Still, sometime in 1961, I was angry enough to yank open the refrigerator door and slam a glass bottle of milk on the shelf. It collided with that same great force into another glass bottle of milk on the shelf. They both broke and milk and glass went everywhere! I had no idea such intensity was in me.

Suddenly aware of the problem, I cleaned the mess and drove alone to the church we attended. At the altar, once again, I gave God everything; my life and my son.

In 1963, our second child was born. A girl. Sheryl Diane. She was born by appointment, a c-section, two weeks before her due date. She was the first girl born into my in-law's family for fifty years. She was special to everyone. My pastor came by the hospital early to have prayer with me.

"She looks like she's going to a party," was his diagnosis to my waiting family.

About that time, a young teen I had come to know from teaching Sunday School came to live with us as a foster child. Connie was sixteen, with background issues of her own. She needed a stable, loving family. I thought we had one!

I was excited to have the girls. I wanted them very badly. Dick, who before marriage, let me know he didn't want children, had little to do with the girls – or so I thought at the time.

However, he had begun investing a little more time in Ken as he got old enough to ask questions about the things Dick found interesting. As a result, Ken learned about aviation, astronomy, electronics, and anything science related while he was still quite young.

I did the normal things; had the normal traumas of life. My siblings experienced their own traumas. At the time, we were not a very close family.

I loved the overnight science field trip to the Museum of Science and Industry in Chicago we took with students as part of Dick's teaching job.

My parents moved to Durango, Colorado for two years, then to McPherson, Kansas. During one visit to them in Durango, we went to the Grand Canyon. I watched with my heart in my throat as Dad carried my small fry daughter on his shoulders right up the edge of the canyon. I imagine he felt sure-footed, but I desperately prayed for their safety.

Ken was in the hospital for two weeks at age two-and a half .... a trauma for any parent.He went through every test imaginable, including a bone marrow test! It was horrible. Then in a couple short years, Ken started started kindergarten. Another trauma! We both cried.

When Ken was eight years old, we received word our two-and half-year-old nephew, Wesley drowned in the family swimming pool. We all felt hurt and devastated beyond belief.

During the next few weeks, I noticed Ken's behavior became unusually gruff. When I confronted him one night, he burst into tears.

With one great sob, he cried out. "Why couldn't it have been me? I'm older. I would've died for him." Only God could comfort us all.

We returned each summer to one of the happy places of my childhood – Cowden Camp Meeting. Again, I made new friends and renewed friendships from earlier camp days. We basked in long talks, prayer times, and laughter. We played innocent pranks on each other and bonded for the long haul.

But Dick and I continued to disagree on nearly Everything...and drifted even more apart.

In 1965, the seemingly secure seams of my life began fraying. We were well established in our town, our church, and Dick in a teaching position in a nearby town. Dick began to change and talk a lot about one particular female student. The town where he taught was a gossipy small town, and rumors began to fly. No one had any proof. There was some truth to the gossip, but no proof.

I knew what was happening that year or two. Sunday dinner was usually spent at the home place with the folks. One particular weekend, this student was our guest, as she was on many weekends.

I was busy peeling potatoes for dinner. As I looked around, I saw Dick's parents enjoying some hugging and kissing. Then I saw Dick standing in front of our guest straightening her bow on the front of her blouse. I thought, "What is wrong with this picture?" But I straightened my mask a little tighter, continued to smile and peel potatoes.

Dick finally resigned his job and found a position in another town.

While going through the motions of moving, I consistently stuffed the feelings of being betrayed and rejected down far below the surface of my life so they wouldn't show in the way I lived or talked. I pulled my happy face on tighter and vowed to keep my marriage and my world together.

Soon rearing children, church activities, and entertaining high school students in my home once again gave meaning to life.

In June 1966, we moved to Arcola, IL for Dick to teach. We were there until 1974.

The summer of 1966, Dick began work on his master's degree in Delaware, OH.

Because I had dealt with the recent past events with a lot of tears, Dick offered to let me go back to Illinois to stay with his parents. I had no desire to do that. My happy face got a bit tighter.

During these winters, both my parents and Dick's lived in Florida, sometimes next to each other. When I visited, Dick's mother was jealous and pouted when I spent time with my parents. My parents, not wanting trouble, would tell me to go back to my in-laws after a short while. 'Vacations' in Florida were not my idea of relaxation.

We purchased a TV shop. I managed it full time for a year while Dick taught school and made service calls in the evening. The kids came to the shop after school.

Dick purchased a Cessna 175, which I tolerated – even enjoyed as we saw a lot of our United States. I used to joke about it being his mistress. Aeronautics was Dick's passion. Ken learned to land the plane at age nine, and enjoyed it immensely. I learned to fly enough to be able to land a plane in an emergency. I still have a logbook.

We spent three summers (1967-1970) in Oxford, Mississippi as Dick finished his master's degree. We lived on one of those stipends universities give to upper level students to encourage them to attend.

In 1967, I tried to buy groceries by writing a check. The store denied me as my name was on their register. I'd had three checks returned. It was my fault through errors in bookkeeping.

It was total humiliation!!!

To make things worse, our pastor's family from Illinois came to visit for the weekend with the news that all our meat had thawed because the electric company had turned off the electricity in our house without notifying us. Connie and other neighbors cleaned up the mess. I did not look forward to seeing the house when we returned home.

Back at home, I got involved with starting the children's ministry. To my delight, it grew! God's presence was often close and precious.

And Connie got married. We had an outside reception. I was very happy. I was happy she was happy in her new marriage. Leroy was the high school football captain and our pastor's son.

Early in 1974, we made a decision to sell the TV Shop and go into ministry. It seemed like the right thing to do. In just a few months our TV business, our van and house sold, leaving use free to enter pastoral ministry.

I didn't question Dick about his 'call' to the ministry. The Ministerial Education and Guidance Board of our denomination (the committee who approves ministerial candidates) didn't ask the questions that would have brought to light our troubled, unresolved marriage issues. A deep, all encompassing desire to follow God and be useful in His service was so much a part of me, it kept me from facing my failure in hiding them.

So, again, my memories are arranged by where we lived.

We pastored in Hillsboro, IL, Effingham, IL, St. Louis, MO (the North County church), and finally, Herrin, IL and Ferges lL.

In the process of being transported to Hillsboro, the couch rolled off the truck, down the interstate, and smashed the whole thing to bits. I was grateful no cars ended up in the path of flying debris, and one lost couch didn't trouble me much.

But the parsonage did. It was awful. In those days, the parsonage was located right next to the church. Rats had taken up residence on the back porch, there were no cupboards, and the sink was horribly stained. We took a two-thirds cut in pay and in life style.

Further discouragement came from a bursitis attack so bad I was virtually useless. The bright spot was the wonderful people who came to help move in.

My parents and Connie stayed several days, arranged furniture, put up drapes, and unpacked. I couldn't reach my right arm high enough to comb my hair.

I finally spent some time in the hospital to treat the bursitis.

The Hillsboro (IL) church put together a 'sunshine box' of remember-forever-magnitude for me while I was in the hospital in Champaign-Urbana (IL) for back surgery. I was there five weeks that time, four hours from home.

It was a terribly tring time in which I leaned heavily upon the Lord. One of my favorite verses was Psalms 56:3, "What time I am afraid I will trust the Lord."

When I came home from the hospital, I was 'kindly' informed by a church member about the rumors concerning Dick circulating. I closed my eyes to it. I didn't want to hear it, or follow up on it. I didn't do anything. *"Who knows the truth of the matter?"* I comforted myself.

Another a bright spot came along with our return to camp meeting. Two friends helped me dress (I was still in a lot of pain.) as well as kept me encouraged.

Following my extended hospital stay in 1975, my outgoing, leader of a daughter became sad, disturbed, and pre-occupied. She didn't want to be touched; our mother-daughter closeness disappeared. Her grades fell. She began fabricating stories about herself, refused to bathe, comb her hair, or wear the nice clothes she once loved. She was eleven years old.

These days the symptoms are fairly well recognized and can be narrowed down to two or three causes, but in those days, we were all at a loss.

Ministry continued while I dealt with her sudden withdrawal. I became more driven to hide my own issues and hurt.

Wade and Ellen Robinson moved from Louisiana to pastor the Litchfield Church of our denomination, just ten miles south, and we reconnected as colleagues.

We moved to Effingham, IL, and my main personal focus narrowed to our daughter's continuing destructive behavior, and a continuing battle to deal with my mother-in-law's chronic negative attitude, especially toward me.

It seemed I never did or said anything right. My feelings of inadequacy clamored for attention but I shoved a lid on them by immersing myself in church work.

Our adventuresome son was growing up. He was outgoing, gregarious, likeable, social, and lived on the edge of adventure. We got him a unicycle and he became an expert. He had a band that met upstairs in the parsonage called Master Mind (before the game was invented). I'll always remember the rendition of Proud Mary they played over and over. And he was into talking on the CB. Midnight Biker was Ken's CB handle. Through his interest in communication, he connected with people all over the world as a ham radio operator.

He was not afraid to be himself, and was a source of joy during these days.

We had pets: a cocker spaniel named Snoopy, a Siamese cat named Dusty, parakeets named Legia and Nigel, and a tarantula named Roselita. There was a menagerie of other varmits Ken called pets.

I cooked for the Head Start Program. The children called me "Cooker."

I had wonderful times with the 'gang' at camp meetings.

We did ministry. We looked normal.

Our daughter was hospitalized for emotional problems of unknown origins to us while we pastored in Saint Louis, North County Free Methodist Church.

Between hospital stays, we went to counseling and part of our routine for 'normalcy' was stopping for White Castle hamburgers on the way home.

But the required family counseling sessions didn't go well. Dick and Ken were more bewildered than anything, and Dick became disconnected from us. He believed no one else needed to be involved.

"Let's be normal," he insisted.

Sheryl did some candy striping at a local hospital, which was good. It was meaningful to her, although her problems continued. She continued to distance herself from people.

Ken graduated from high school and went to Greenville College, where his grandfather, aunt, uncle, and I had attended. His outgoing personality continued and he easily made friends. He was disc jockey for the campus radio station, and took pictures for the yearbook. Not surprisingly, his major was communications.

He's always loved bikes. The unicycle has gotten him into parades and even on television.

But to us, in the pastorate, it was slowly becoming apparent we didn't fit in well in the very white collar, city church of North County Church. However, we made life long friends with a couple in the church. Glenn Palone was in the Air Force. Together, with his wife, Leta, they lent strong support, and we became life-long friends. Glenn was influential in Ken's decision to have a career in the Air Force.

Then our church conference appointment committee moved us to Herrin, in Southern Illinois.

The Herrin house was the same one I lived in as a child … and I met older versions of many of the same people. It was like homecoming. My favorite Sunday School teacher was old, but still alive. She had given me a glass slipper for memorizing scripture in 1949.

Our daughter's hospitalizations continued. We traveled back and forth to St. Louis to counseling and hospitals. Her suicide attempts continued, and emergencies filled my emotional life. It usually happened on weekends, or around Christmas holidays. When she was sixteen, a psychiatrist told me she would spend her adult life in an institution.

"No way!" I told myself and a close friend. I felt a deep anger that insisted I do something. The question was, of course, "What?"

In 1981, we arranged for her to spend the last two years of high school at Oakdale, which is a small Christian High School in the hills of Kentucky. God sent us there to save all our lives. For that time, we were surrounded with love, prayers, and support from the staff.

Ministry continued. I took a friend to Springfield, IL, for chemotherapy every two weeks, and stayed when she had surgery. I directed children's camps for three summers. I cultivated friendships. A young man of twenty-six or so made it a habit to come by the parsonage early for coffee and conversation nearly every morning. I continued to do church, driven by the need to be busy.

We spent several Christmases with a couple who were part of our church, and also friends. Their fireplace and fellowship were always warm and cozy. I felt and reflected it all, and soaked up the hospitality they offered.

However, most of those Christmases, Dick seemed unusually angry and indifferent. He couldn't seem to get into the spirit of sharing Christmas with friends.

Ken graduated from college and joined the Air Force. He chose to be stationed in England. He later confessed – which is the word he used – "I wanted to get away from the crazy family and start one of my own." That he did, getting married early in his time in England.

I helped our daughter-in-law-to-be get ready for her wedding, get a passport for her trip to England, and shop for gifts for with her mother, Nancy, who continues to be a good friend.

One shopping day in St. Louis it was drizzling rain and we circled the parking lot looking for that one open space. We saw it on the other side of the lot. Nancy jumped out of the car and ran to the space. She stood, occupying the spot, in the drizzle, until I drove around to it. Although wet, she enjoyed the spontaneity of the moment.

Sheryl graduated from Oakdale! A convoy of three cars of relatives went for the ceremony. I was so happy I cried. What an achievement!

I wondered if she would want to attend college, and if she did, if she would make it.

In 1983, we took a wonderful trip to England for two weeks. During our time there, we planned an overnight in Brugge, Belgium. The evenng before, I had gone alone to the bakery in Banbury to purchase some sweets to eat quickly before we left. Ther clerk couldn't understand English, and I couldn't understand her. I pointed to a variety of delicacies for us to enjoy in the middle of the night, 3AM, to hold us until we could get a proper breakfast.

"Yuck!" I exclaimed when I bit into one.

It was a meat pie! Since I'd left them out overnight, it landed in the garbage. It wasn't my idea of a sweet treat.

In spits of meat at 3 AM, we did successfully board a Jet Foil and rode across the English Channel. It was a totally awesome, fun ride.

I enjoyed the walks in Brugge's narrow brick streets, and the delicious coffee and chocolate the staff brought to our room on a tray in the hotel.

In England, I had the inevitable language mix-up. As so many people have discovered, napkins there are not what they are here. I'd bought some donuts and sweet rolls for a snack, but forgot to bring napkins. In the midst an elbow-to-elbow crowd, jostling along, I spotted a small market.

In my clear voice that carries really well, I made a request of Ken. "If you would go and get us some napkins, we'll go to the car and have do-nuts."

Ken's flushed face was turning from me, as he quickened his pace to deny he even knew who I was. Of course, I learned I should have asked for serviettes. In England, napkins are used by females once a month. We call them menstrual pads.

But, there are a lot of good memories from that trip.

Soon after the trip, a series of life changing events began when I began work as a volunteer chaplain at Marion Hospital. There is no doubt for me God worked through me there. It was a time of affirmation and growth.

One day, I was giving reassurance to a female patient. I offered to pray for her before I left.

"Are you qualified to do that?" she asked in all sincerity.

"Yes," I answered honestly, and we prayed.

However, she brought to the surface my deep longing to be more involved in the pastoral ministry on a professional level. I contacted the conference superintendent and relayed the incident, expressing my desire to be 'qualified.'

He gave me instruction and I began correspondence courses with Asbury Seminary and our denominational headquarters. I began studies for Deacon's orders. At that time, it was the first step toward final ordination. I thought I had the blessings of my husband, parents, and conference superintendent. The conference appointed me assistant to my husband in pastoral ministry.

After some ups and downs, our daughter went to Central College to study psychology.

We experienced some difficult years in our ministry of the two-circuit church appointment to Herrin and Ferges. The members of the two churches had a history of jealousy. However, we became close to the families in both churches.

One family's marriage was much like ours – domineering, controlling husbands with dark moods, and wives caught in the middle. I was drawn to the husband who was the musician at the church because of his love for music. And I loved his wife like a sister.

Nothing, other than me being filled with guilt, happened between the husband and I. But it made Dick extremely angry, and I became more and more aware of the deep, emotional emptiness in my life. I needed acceptance more than I needed sex. My husband fulfilled the sexual part of our marriage without the emotional closeness I longed for.

Overall, though, I was snug on the pastorate. I had a place, appreciation, acceptance, a position, and all my people were in the area. I was doing what I was supposed to do.

The Herrin and Ferges churches had been separated, with each having its own pastor, the year before we went to England. (1982) We were assigned to the Ferges church. We moved into a newly built parsonage. I chose the kitchen furnishings as well as the colors, and drapes. I settled in, somewhat content.

Sometime in 1983, Dick began having symptoms of an unknown illness. He developed a cough so bad we were concerned he'd die during a spell. I insisted, and we began seeking medical help.

By this time, Sheryl quit Central College in Kansas and returned home.

In October of 1984, we went to Greenville College for a ministerial conference. One message that stuck was about Abraham being called by God to leave his place, his position, and people.

"A powerful sermon for anyone needing it," I thought.

Back at the Ferges parsonage, the phone was ringing as we walked in the door. The dean of our denominational college in McPherson, Kansas was calling to offer my husband a teaching position in science and aeronautics.

He wanted to accept on the spot. However, he deferred to me. I couldn't say no. One of his desires had always been to teach in one of our denominational colleges.

We had lived in that beautiful new parsonage less than two years.

God had sent the Abraham message as an "A-ha" moment for me.

That ended our ministry together. Other than the children, it's all we really had in common.

CHAPTER SIX

REFLECTIONS ON COLLEGE AND MARRIAGE CINDY ROBINSON

My two years of college were so short and filled with terror and tension, I don't think about them much. I must have looked somewhat acceptable to other students. I had 'friends'. Acquaintances mostly, though. I dated a couple of boys. I passed classes.

I paid no attention to the most significant thing of my college years; Professor Beeson who, in his wisdom, tried to warn me about my marriage.

And he was right. Dick came from a more liberal background. I came from a very conservative one. My professor didn't, nor do I, judge the value of either stance. But he recognized something I didn't. At eighteen years of age, I didn't know the differences would be my unmaking. He also knew, and I didn't, my new family would try to shape me into the "their mold."

Even my name changed. Once I moved to New York, I was no longer Florine. They called me Cindy. I've been Cindy ever since.

Although I conformed to my fiancée's family's ways of doing things, the 'becoming one in spirit' never happened, which was a gut wrenching thing for me through the years. We were never good friends to laugh, to worship or to play together.

From my point of view, Dick didn't 'court' me. He didn't ask for dates. He just assumed I'd be there. There was no romance. While romance isn't everything, and I could have adjusted, his attitude of assuming I'd be there carried into our marriage.

Looking back, I realize the marriage was built on deception and parental approval.

But the deception was more than Dick's indiscreet behavior. On my side, the marriage was born of the need to be needed, and a fear no one else would ever want me, rather than on lasting, mutual caring love and friendship.

I didn't tell anyone except my sister about my internal battles with Dick's behavior. I determined to make Dick's home his castle (as we used to say). I spent the next thirty years doing that, as though his behavior was my fault.

I read the Bible avidly, had devotions, wanted to do right, and was active in church work.

I found only guilt and unhappiness. When Dick behaved indiscreetly with someone, I somehow had caused it. God was there, but I only knew the God of my father and other ministers of that era; legalistic, judging and punishing every error, and every unpleasant thought I had. My guilt over not telling anyone I knew what was happening was nearly unforgivable.

Yet, often, I felt God's presence in services. These were usually at camp meetings, times away from my normal life. They gave me hope. And they helped me through my return to normal life.

The long days in the hospital after my back surgery were days to try my soul and my faith. One of the verses I pulled out of the Sunshine box our church had sent was Psalm 56:3 "What time I am afraid, I will trust in the Lord."

On the flip side of that, was a church member who brought me a book to read. The basic 'truth' of the book was if I claimed more faith, God would heal me.

God knows I claimed everything I knew to claim, but the place I ended up was "Thy will be done."

In daily life, I continued to battle guilt. I grew weary of the negative words that populated my relationship with my mother-in-law. I would go so far and have to repent of my feelings. I would start over, only to end up repenting again.

My mother-in-law and I had a clash of values. It seemed to me we disagreed on most things. For instance, a big thing was how I parented my children and managed my household. I often felt her displeasure and knew she didn't want Dick to marry me in the first place. He stayed out of our conflicts. From the time we married until the end, I spent a lot of time crying and praying for grace in the relationship with my Mother-in-law.

Finally, my father-in-law let me know I wasn't alone. "If you want to get along, you will have to change. She will never change."

I wanted to keep peace, but could not change my values. The pressure kept me spiritually crying out to God.

By the time we had entered the ministry, I had learned how not to feel. What I had really learned was how to deny that I felt.

I felt anyway, but stuffed it so far down inside, and convinced myself I didn't feel. Dick hated tears. He completely ignored me when I was sad or tearful. I came to assume God felt the same way.

I learned the dull ache and void of feeling betrayed could be covered over with activities of life. I concentrated on raising the kids, church work, and at one point, I even started babysitting in the home. But even those activities sometimes added to the hurt.

One infant I took care of was Jaleana. She was left in my care five days a week for two years.

We grew attached to her and she to us. She was like our own. One weekend, unknown to me, she asked her mother to leave her at my house. Her mother felt that would be an imposition on me. But without checking with me, she allowed her to visit her aunt in a nearby town. As the aunt was returning home with Jalena on Monday, the car broadsided an oncoming train. Jalena and her aunt were killed.

Once again, our family grieved the death of a little one. And once again, Ken wondered why he couldn't have taken her place.

I searched my own life and felt totally committed to whatever God wanted for us. I read the Bible and prayed as if my life depended on that. I guess, in a way, it did.

Also, I'd become such a wimpy person, I couldn't address any difficult situation truthfully. I had to shade truth, it seemed, to keep peace, or be non-committal. I just took whatever my mother-in-law, Dick, and unhealthy relationships I encountered in our churches dished out. It seemed to me every time I spoke truth it backfired.

From the beginning of our marriage, Dick told me he wasn't a people person, but a practical scientific type person. As our pastorate continued, our people sensed it, and came to me with their needs.

On the extreme opposite end, I needed people. I needed them so much it was unhealthy. I thrived on their need of me. Yet, I was able to unfailingly encourage others in their faith.

I was numb; hanging onto a faith that God would take care of us. A miracle would happen, God would rescue me, and heal our marriage. Meanwhile, I put on a happy face. No one knew my internal struggles as I kept busy.

All the time, the external ministry activities went on. After a troubled daughter was added to the mix, I just added her to my load of worry, activity list, and guilt over whatever caused her illness. I knew it must be my fault.

Both men and women affirmed me during this time. I was hungry for attention, for nurture, and love for being me. It hadn't been a part of my life growing up, and not part of my marriage. I bloomed under compliments and care. Some families along the way accepted me and included me as part of their family.

From being around other families, I began to wonder if Dick simply didn't know how to give love and care. Was it that he didn't know anything else to do, so he put more and more distance between us? Was he as frustrated as I was? I still don't know.

I well remember one Sunday morning at Herrin about 1982 or so, singing a chorus "He's All

I Need." I was ashamed to confess my thought…
"Lord, I need friends too."

My sin, for which I continually sought forgiveness, was to keep the secrets.

When the MEG board didn't ask the questions that would bring out the troubles and our disconnected marriage, I didn't give a hint that something was wrong in my life. As our ministry continued, I covered up for Dick's sharp, unkind attitude to church members. I was good at spinning his words to make him appear the kind, loving, giving pastor I wanted us both to be.

I kept our daughter's illness a secret. The church people saw its symptoms in the distance she put between her and everyone, but had no idea of the despair she and I felt. I kept a hope before me in the form imagining an office, a desk, and her name plaque on it. This held me through the hard times.

It seems a tremendous contradiction, but all through our ministry, God kept me close. He gave me strength. He kept me together. He kept Ken from mortal emotional scars, with his outgoing and gregarious personality intact. God was able to bless people through me/us, and did not desert me. Ever.

All that from a legalistic, demanding God whose standards were so high I could never reach them, no matter how much I did. I fluctuated between guilt and thanksgiving.

Imagine how I felt when I found grace and mercy!

CHAPTER SEVEN

END OF A MARRIAGE
CINDY ROBINSON

December 31, 1984, we moved to McPherson, Kansas with the intent to teach at Central College a few years, and then return to the classrooms of Illinois for ten or so years to enhance Dick's retirement.

I was physically ill from mourning and weeping, I couldn't drive. We had a caravan of vehicles. Sheryl took over driving mine through the snowy weather that had turned into an icy blizzard. From my bed in the back seat, through the fog of a sedative, I could hear a good friend on his CB coaching Sheryl in her driving. Thank God for caring friends and the CB's of the eighties!

Quietly, he would say, "You're doing a great job, Sheryl." And then reassure her with other words I don't remember so clearly.

However, once we got there, a Sunday school class in McPherson left their New Year's Eve party to help us get in. Conditions on that end were also wintry and dangerous.

The dean of Central College was upset about the house – he thought we could do better. It was a bit of a cracker box - all we could find on such short notice. But we settled in and Dick began teaching January 1985.

The summer of 1985, in Greenville, IL, I received my Deacons orders. I was also the guest speaker at the Central Illinois ladies' retreat. I learned how to get back and forth to and from Illinois alone, after touring Kansas City a couple of times before figuring out where to exit and head north. I wasn't too upset about touring KC without really meaning to. It was a reality in my traveling. I often took the scenic route!

With the distance between Dick and me growing, I began doing a lot on my own without really knowing what I was doing.

We did church. Our daughter enrolled at Central. She graduated in 1986, however, she was suspended twice and was required to have counseling.

Dick was not supportive in any part of Sheryl's recovery. He had little faith in the counseling process.

This time, however, the cause of her illness began to come out, and the counselors targeted her treatment to rape recovery. We never determined the exact circumstances. We may never know the whole truth.

But we did learn one abuser was a neighbor, the father of her best girl friend. I later learned her perpetrator told her "If you ever tell, your mother won't love you anymore," and "If you tell, it will go worse for you than for me."

She believed his lies.

Through the years of turmoil, God had taken care of her, providing counselors to get her to that point, where she could finally tell her secret. Some of her sounselors even charged as little as five dollars a session.

My response when we finally got to the cause was "Now we can get help." Dick's was "Now we can put it behind us and get on with life."

I admitted Sheryl to St. John's inpatient psychiatric facility for a month, and she earnestly began the road to recovery.

Rumors of Dick's indiscreet behavior began again. While he admitted to some, I shut my eyes to others. My marriage was forever.

I continued to feel Dick's anger. I remember one night after the Sunday evening service I went to the altar to pray. When I got up, Dick was coming down the aisle from outside with a very angry face. He wanted the keys to our daughter's car.

"He doesn't love me." The thought struck me numb. My spiritual needs didn't mean anything to him, and it hurt deeply.

On we went.

I realized it was a good time to do what I felt I wanted and enrolled in college to finish my college education. I was new to the state of Kansas, our children were grown, and Dick was teaching the subjects of his passion. With the help of a guidance counselor at Central College, I took the unexpected opportunity to finish my own college degree. I chose social work and began to pursue it at Bethany College located in Lindsborg, Kansas, twenty miles away.

My return to college added another level of conflict to our marriage. Dick didn't contribute to my education emotionally or financially. He wanted me home.

"There wouldn't be anyone there to fix my lunch," he complained.

I worked part time at the Christian Counseling Center and the Central College cafeteria. These were good times for me. I worked with some very wonderful people.

In 1988 -1989, I was appointed pastor of the Hutchinson Kansas Free Methodist Church. It was a busy, very good year. I finished my college and graduated in 1989. I again found people who affirmed me; a place to serve where I felt I made a difference.

I thrived in the pastorate. But two things interfered with my continuing: I had finished my college and was ready to start a career in social work, and Dick's health had continued to deteriorate bit by bit.

He still resisted treatment until he had no choice. We had begun making trips to the Mayo Clinic in Rochester, MN. I couldn't work, travel to Mayo, and pastor. My energies wouldn't stretch that far.

Trips to the clinic and my new career at Moundridge Memorial Home as the social worker became the focus of life.

We continued to do church activities. My faith never wavered, and I could see God at work in my life. But no matter how much life handed me outside of church, the God I knew sat down standards that demanded I do SOMETHING at church.

Dick was finally given a diagnosis: sarcoidosis. It's the result of an overactive immune system. Trips for treatment followed as Dick and I both continued our careers.

But in May of 1989, the disease attacked his central nervous system, and he was forced to quit teaching and working. He had to have a walker to move around, and periodically, a wheelchair. In August, he had a TIA (mini-stroke). We made about twenty trips to Rochester that year.

With Dick's inability to work and me in a new career, God had to provide somehow. He did so in the form of help from family and our church friends. We would not have survived otherwise.

Life went on, but I was changing. My study in social work became the tool through which God revealed the emotional and physical *'dis-ease'* in my own life. A personal developmental stages of life. A journal was a requirement in one of my classes, and God opened my eyes to spiritual and emotional truths I'd never before considered.

But it seemed the closer I got to God, the more distance Dick put between us. We were at opposite ends of a great chasm without anything to bridge the gap.

As a result of my growth, I began initiating conversations with Dick during the long trips to Rochester, attempting to get him to talk to me.

Once, early on, he stated he gave our marriage five years.

"I'll never divorce you," I promised.

On October 1, 1990, I was driving on the way home from a trip to Illinois. I asked. "What do you want in marriage?"

"Whatever." He went to sleep while I drove with tears in my eyes and hurt in my heart as I pondered what was happening. When he woke up, we resumed the conversation.

"What do you want in marriage?" I asked again.

"What do you want?" He turned the question to me.

"Spiritual fellowship, prayer together, emotional support, working together in the home with chores. Now, what do you want?"

"You need to change people," he replied. I understood he was saying I needed another man…. Change partners. "You've been nice to me for thirty years."

"No. That's not the solution," I insisted. "We need to change and grow in the situation."

That was the end of the conversation. I was left to drive and think about what he said.

During this time, I came to understand human needs and what people will do when a marriage relationship doesn't meet basic emotional needs. My social work training and the job experience opened my eyes to dysfunctional realities in my life.

There were people I have 'attached' to in my years of ministry - both with my husband, and after he began teaching college, as I pastored alone. They were people who affirmed me and helped meet emotional needs Dick couldn't.

Dick knew I had not sought a physical relationship outside marriage, nor did I want one. Yet Dick misunderstood these relationships. He called them 'emotional adultery.' I had never heard or thought of that concept. At the time, I thought I had close friends. "Crusades" is the word Dick used.

It wasn't until I understood these things, that God could finally help me. God finally revealed to me my way of relating was not always healthy. I wouldn't have understood what I was doing before all this took place.

But I did come to know part of what was wrong with the marriage was my responsibility. I began asking Dick to go to counseling with me. He firmly said 'no' to attending any of the Marriage Encounters that were being held in our area. I began counseling alone. In 1991, I got a "if you think it is necessary," from Dick, and we entered counseling together.

At the end of ten sessions the counselor, a pastor, marriage and family therapist, and Godly man, confronted Dick about not expending any energy on his marriage, nor trying to work on it. Dick let the counselor know it was entirely my problem, not his. He quit at that point.

I continued, facing my own issues as God revealed them.

On a different level, through the years I slowly had become Dick's caretaker. Even with our marriage a silent battleground, he asked more and more of me in terms of taking care of his physical needs. And I suppose, I still needed to be needed. I seemed to be driven by an inner need to know and be known.

Our son returned to the States and was stationed in California. I traveled there twice to visit him and his growing family. Our daughter graduated from Greenville College with a BA, and began her own
journey to wholeness.

This was a major event for both of us. It was another step toward that office and name plaque on a desk.

Around 1986 Wade and Ellen Robinson's son came to Central College for his first two years of college before going on to Greenville. Aviation was his interest, which is what Dick taught. He was in and out of our home for a couple of years, even staying with us for a short time. His parents visited occasionally, driving from their Louisiana home. They stayed in our home during these visits.

Life was busy. I continued in the error of enduring the anger, demands, and lack of nurture in the marriage, while reading the Bible passionately, doing church, encouraging everyone in their faith, and putting on my everything's-just-fine face for everyone outside my house. Only my counselors and close friends knew about the long walks and bike rides I took to be alone to cry out to God. Or the nights I cried myself to sleep.

A friend of mine, Sally, was with me on one of those bike rides. I was so overcome with tears we had to pull over. We plopped on the ground. I sobbed, and Sally sang quietly to me. God provided enough healing for me to go on.

By 1991, Dick's illness was under control, so the visits to Mayo Clinic ended for a short time. He continued on a low dose of prednisone, but in August 1992, he began coughing again. We all knew what that meant; the beginning of the end.

August 10th, Dick took the unusual step of initiating a conversation.

"I've decided not to go back to Mayo Clinic," he said. "I'm just going to let nature take its course."

My heart froze since I knew well what that meant. "Do you want to talk to your parents or the pastor?" I asked, remembering he had calmed down and listened to his father when he was out of control over the repayment of his college bills many years earlier.

"No."

"Do you want tp talk to the pastor?"

"No, not until closer to the end." His tone closed the conversation.

In my total distress, I called my counselor the next day. He made time for me, and we dealt with the very painful reality. I came to the decision to quit making things easy for Dick. I also came to understand he needed space to make a clear decision without my presence clouding the issues.

The questions I had to ask were:

    1. Could I morally stay around and make it easy for him to die?

    2. Did he really want to die?

With prayer and guidance, I concluded it was time for me to leave.

The morning I moved thirty miles south to Newton, Kansas, I told Dick why I was leaving. He didn't ask if there was anything he could do, or what went wrong. Within five minutes, he made three statements.

"We will have to divide things up."

"We will have to see about a divorce."

"We will need to sell the house."

I refuted all three of them. "We need time to think. I want to talk about reconciliation."

"It's your fault," was his only reply.

I wrote the following letter:

August 15, 1992

Dear Family and Friends,

After months of professional Christian counseling, Dick has made the decision to passively commit suicide by discontinuing his medical treatment. There is a very inexpensive medication available that will enhance his quality of life and longevity if he should wish to take it. I am sharing with you this statement of his choice un-der the direction of a Christian counselor who has worked with both Dick and me.

I refuse to assist or to enable him in this behav-ior. Therefore, I am moving to my own apartment. This in no way closes any doors to possible recon-ciliation. As you know, my values are commitment to relationship, to marriage, and to wholesome life.

You are well aware, the problems are not all one-sided. The problems are long-standing and have been left for many years without resolution.

The personal side of this is that I've spent many hours with the Lord seeking His help, His guid-ance, love, and forgiveness. I covet your prayers for both Dick and me; we will need them. I know that God is still in the business of reconciling lives.

Thank you for all being gracious and support-ive. In Christian love,
Cindy

I sent the letter to the members of the Sunday School class I was teaching as well as family mem-bers and close friends. But instead of sending a let-ter to my parents, I sent it to my sister and asked her to read it to my parents. They were getting old enough I didn't want them to read the letter without a friendly face to be with them. I gave them two weeks and called my father.

"You are the aggressor here," he stated. "You should stay with him. Give him another chance."

He agreed with Dick. It was all my fault. Forty minutes or so later, I hung up the phone numb with bone-tiredness, shame, and hurt. He heaped hurt upon hurt and added guilt.

I did give Dick another chance. I asked for reconciliation three times. The first was August 17th, when I moved out. The second time was October 6th, with a friend in attendance for witness.

"Do you need more time to think and sort things out?" I asked.

"Well, I don't think there is anymore that can be done. I don't like unfinished things. We need to make a clean break to let me get on with my life. We need to get a divorce."

I talked to him again October 26th, and asked if he would consider reconciliation.

"No. I've talked to an attorney, who will draw the papers up. I'll go file on Monday."

Since 1986, Dick had thrown labels at me that included humanist, feminist, and even lesbian. Said in private, they hurt, and made me feel misunderstood and unloved. Now he went public with the lesbian label.

People approached my mother or me to check out the truth of the rumor. It went to Lakeland, FL to Michigan, then to Iowa, and New York. Who knows where else?

I had even resigned my job under allegations as my boss believed my husband's rumors. (God provided another job.)

A mutual friend from Iowa was in Newton for a meeting late in 1992 and called to invite me to breakfast. He couldn't discuss what he had on his mind over the phone. At breakfast he was so embarrassed, I made it easy for him.

"I know what the rumors are," I opened the conversation. I have no idea how long we talked.

Finally, he nodded. "I believe you, and I am so sad for Dick."

Certainly, there was no truth to the rumor. I had determined, however, not to defend myself until friends inquired of me. I still value both my close male and female friends who, through the years, have provided a stability and saneness not available to me in my marriage.

In the end, the fracture of our marriage wasn't totally about Dick's indiscretions. It had more to do with being discounted as a person, with being shut out of my husband's life, and his wanting to die rather than live with me. Dick often turned on three TV sets simultaneously rather than, it seemed to me, have a conversation with me.

"If you can talk about airplanes, computers, or science, we'll talk," had summed it all up for him.

Dick moved to Illinois the summer of 1993. The divorce was final May 25, 1993 – just short of five years after he told me he gave the marriage five years.

That fall he met a woman, announced their engagement at a New Year's Eve Party at church, and married April 3, 1994. He was also given a clean bill of health and got back his pilot's license.

It was over. I was on my own. I continued counseling. God was faithful as I sought forgiveness for my foolishness and my part of the failure of the marriage.

Sanctuary
By Cindy

Open the doors of my soul
Let the Sounds of nature
The sights and smells
Enter into the core of me.
So many sounds
Birds calling to birds
traffic going from east to west
and from west to east again.
People sounds nearby
Also out to enjoy nature.
The space you gave me, Lord,
is indeed a living sanctuary.
May the sights, sounds and smells
That go out of me
Be my living sacrifice of praise to
You –
A living sacrifice!

Intimacy
By Cindy

Sweep away the cobwebs of my mind
Shovel out past garbage
Clear out the debris
Cut through the muddling
And form prayers from the back roads of my
                                                          mind.

Prayers of praise and gratitude
To bring you honor and glory
Intimacy
I want to be close to you
I want to know your Presence
I want your will to shadow me
Only to abandon myself to you.
Intimacy
To know and be known – fully.
Make me still thirsty
To drink forever deeply in
The wells of your romance.

CHAPTER EIGHT

REFLECTIONS
CINDY ROBINSON

The years from 1987 through 1992 were like a conversion to me: a whole new opening of myself.

It began with the process of God gradually revealing the dark sides of my heart and life through my studies. I also learned a great deal from my daughter as she struggled with her issues. She taught me the meaning of the word 'codependent."

As early as 1990, I had identified essential qualities in a relationship, and realized my marriage had very few, if any of them:

Communication / Affection / Compassion / Forgiveness / Honesty /Acceptance / Dependability / Sense of humor /Romance / Patience / and Freedom.

As I studied, I discovered the God of grace and love who had been there all the time, eclipsed most of the time by the image of the judge God of my life. I discovered I didn't have to be bound by legalistic rules, attempting to live up to an impossible standard of being and doing, while all the time pleasing everyone.

But I also realized without ministry during my marriage, I may not have survived.

I am grateful for that ministry, but it was about the wrong thing. It was about doing, being needed, being known as a problem solver, and hiding secrets.

God began healing my driven soul.

For the first two years, my first counselor and I worked on resolving childhood issues while working on the marriage relationship until he moved out of the area. Then, after Dick's short participation and refusal to face anything, I continued for five more years with another counselor.

June 27, 1992, about two months before the final separation, I'd come to a realization that many men and women (more often than men, I think) never realize. I wrote the following entry in my journal:

I just can't go back to the old way of being super woman, wife, and mother. When I'm obsessed with everyone else's troubles and I'm mothering an adult male, I really have nothing of lasting value to give. I cannot give what I do not have. If I don't have peace, nurture, and affirmation, I can't give (them). I can't give myself if I have no self to give. I wish Dick would journey with me and enjoy the way.

During counseling, God changed me in so many ways, it's almost impossible to know when the final person I am emerged. I had no further need to reach out in unhealthy ways for nurture and affirmation. God gave me Himself. He became everything to me. He truly became all I needed.

I think one of the most difficult things I dealt with was the pain of telling my parents. I had always so wanted to be like my father in his stable spirituality, it nearly killed me when he couldn't understand.

I had spent so many years hiding any inner struggle from them; he could not comprehend what caused all this … all the sudden. I think he was afraid I had walked out on my values and my belief in God. He was, I think, as I look at it in retrospect afraid for my soul. It was so unlike his stable, religious, loving daughter. He didn't know I hadn't been most of those things for a long time.

After I moved out, I began opening more of myself up to God. He sent two women who were going through the same studies as me. One was the Twelve Step Program used by AA.

Together the three of us explored and encountered God at deeper levels. At one of these sessions, one of my friends said to me, "Cindy, you are a driven person."

Ouch, that stung! Even when a dear friend said it in love. Partly in jest, I answered. "Surely, not! Not me."

Just a few evenings later, as I sat relaxing in my apartment, my eye caught a rapid movement. As I watched intently and with utter fascination, a baby mouse raced around the baseboard of the small combination living room and kitchen. I couldn't believe what I was seeing. Surely, my eyes were deceiving me. I felt suspended as for several minutes, I watched and allowed the Holy Spirit to say "Cindy, there you are my driven daughter. Pat is right. Now let me lead you into a slower life style."

That was the first, last, and only mouse I had while living ten years in the Heatheridge Apartments.

God provided a big fish for Jonah, but provided a baby mouse for me. Life began to change and take on a still deeper meaning at a slower pace.

For instance, something as simple as reading God's word changed. I devoured it in a new way. Instead of reading it to prove how devout I was, I read it to learn about God. To worship!

I was learning where "being's" place was in my life and where "doing" belonged.

Solitude
by Cindy

Lord to learn solitude
    And quietness
That is the task.
So much mental muddling
    Unanswered questions
Fears and resentments,
    Whys and wherefores
Demand attention, demand control.
Lord to learn solitude
    And Quietness
That is the task.

Psalm 63:1, 7-8
O God, you are my god
Earnestly I seek you
My soul thirsts for you
My body longs for you
I sing in the shadow of your wings
My soul clings to you
Your right hand upholds me.

Know me deeply, God
Understand the very core
Longings of my heart
Stir your sacred romance in me
Let me know you deeply O God

Your will, Your way, Your laughter
Your love, Your heart
Walking and talking with you
Is my desire
A cup of tea, if you please
Come in and sup with me
Or sit in silence and bask in your romance.

CHAPTER NINE

MARRIAGE AND MINISTRY
WADE ROBINSON

I went to Greenville College in Greenville, IL right out of high school, and took my pre-conceived notions and the judgmental attitude of the day with me.

I could tell who was a Christian and who wasn't by the way they dressed, or how they looked. If girls wore make-up, jewelry, or specific style of clothes, they couldn't be Christians. I thank God my time at college helped modify many of the ideas I took with me.

But one thing it did not modify was my love for Ellen Luttrull. We were already engaged by the time I set off for two years of college, and that love endured.

June 7, 1957, Ellen and I were married, and we headed back to Greenville for another semester.

I served a church called Halford Chapel in 1957 and 1958, but the sights and sounds – and the deep-fried catfish – of the South pulled our hearts back. Besides, Ellen lost her job, and gave us a built in excuse to go home.

The call of God to the ministry remained upon my life, so we accepted appointment to the

Free Methodist church in Oak Grove, where Ellen and I had first met. We also hunted desperately for jobs to supplement the income as the money just wasn't stretching around the needs.

We pastored at Provencal, and Chickasaw, Louisiana in the Gulf Coast Conference (Louisiana) and I was ordained deacon in 1961. In those days Deacon was the first of two ordination levels.

Three years later, I received a shock. Until recent years, conference often held shocks for Free Methodist pastors. You didn't know if you were going to be reappointed or moved to another church until they read the appointments at the end of the annual business meeting of the conference. (Some denominations call them districts.)

When my name was read off in 1964, they said "Wade Robinson, supernumery." If you don't know what that word means, it means "above the number needed." In other words, they didn't have a place for me.

Instantly I was deeply hurt and felt unnecessary, rejected, and betrayed. It was another blow to my self-esteem. I did not plead my case and, since I felt unwanted, left the conference in anger. Later I repented of that anger.

God provided an assistant pastor's position in McAllen, Texas. I was forced to pursue other jobs to supplement the income. I needed to provide for my family. We were in the Rio Grande Valley for three years and once again felt the lure of home. So we returned to Louisiana and took the position of Assistant Pastor in Pineville, LA.

In 1968, we completed our family when Dale was born and joined his siblings, Marvin and Dorothy Grace. I was always afraid of having children for fear they would not become Christians. But their presence in our lives overcame any fear I had. They gave life so much meaning and joy.

However, as in most families, our children had their share of struggles.

In their teen years, a friend of Marvin's named Arnie stopped by to see him.

"Would you like to see Liddieville?" He asked.

So Arnie drove Marvin around the loop, about three miles and started back to the parsonage. Within sight of home, the car started flipping end over end, throwing Arnie out of it, and coming to rest "bottom upwards."

Arnie was killed instantly. Marvin crawled out where the back glass had been. He went to Arnie and found him taking his last breath. The devastation made an impact on all our family.

As we pastored, I felt the need to grow in the pastoral ministry and become a more effective leader in the church. I felt the need to take the final step of ordination and become an Elder in the Free Methodist Church. So, in 1975, God had worked through the events of life and I packed up my family and headed back to Greenville College.

While attending college, I was to serve the Free Methodist church in Litchfiled, IL. When we arrived, a neighboring pastor and his son came to help us unload the U-Haul. By the end of the day, we were tired and our new friend invited us home for the evening meal. When we entered their home, his wife came from the kitchen to welcome us. We recognized each other as classmates in 1955, our freshman year at Greenville.

During the next year, our children became friends and did many things together. Our church congregations also had social activities together often. The pastor and wife were Dick and Cindy. Following that year our friends moved.

The two years at Litchfield took their toll on the family, especially the children. We had uprooted them from their southern ways and friends and placed them in an environment where they didn't know anyone.

It was toughest on Marvin and Dorothy. I made the mistake of allowing Dorothy to be placed in the slow learner class. I did not realize this was equated with having mental disabilities. Even though she is a smart person and she should not have been classified as mentally disabled, it left its mark on her.

The high school they attended was drug infested. It seemed as if other teenagers did not welcome them. They made fun of their southern ways and excluded them from activities.

So, in 1977, things happened very rapidly at the end of our stay in Litchfield. I had completed the requirements for ordination and became an Ordained Elder in our denomination. Marvin graduated high school on a Friday night in May. We loaded the U-Haul on Saturday and I preached my last sermon on Sunday. Early Monday morning, I stomped "the dust" off my feet; we climbed into our vehicles at daylight and headed south. I was glad to get back where I belonged. When we crossed the Louisiana line, I stopped the car and kissed the ground!

So, once again, we returned to the pastorate in the small churches of Louisiana.

The churches were not only small in numbers, they were small in salary. One church had nearly no salary, but provided groceries. I kept a record of the groceries and salary, and, unless my records are wrong, I averaged Thirteen dollars per week. That was groceries and salary combined. The next year my family and I moved to another church and got a big raise. We received thirty-five dollars a week!

So, I pastored, helped Ellen as much as I could with the children, and worked outside the church.

I worked the cotton fields (again!). I worked as a carpenter's helper and electrician's apprentice. Eventually I became a salesman. At one time or another I sold insulation, shoes at Sears, hardware, and men's and boys' clothes at JC Penny's. I worked at Dresser industries making valves. I was a third shift supervisor at a company that made cable. I was a substitute teacher for three different Parishes from K to 12th grades. I worked as delivery man for Sears, delivering and installing appliances. Eventually, I repaired, sold and delivered appliances as my own business.

And through all this, I was spending time preparing sermons and doing the work of the church.

The family did have a diversion ... deer hunting. I bagged my first deer after I'd married into a family of deer hunters. We didn't kill just for sport. They were a major source of our meat. I killed my first deer with my childhood 12-guage.

My sons are also avid hunters. They are better hunters than I am. I started taking Marvin hunting with me when he was three years old. My daughter has bagged more than one deer. Both she and Dale have exciting deer stories to tell.

I remember hunting with Marvin one day in midwinter. The wind was blowing fiercely and the temperature was a chilling thirty degrees. Thankfully, we had a heater in the stand. (A tall metal or wood structure – as fancy or plain as you want it – in the trees where hunters sit to hide from and spot deer.) Finally, a small "legal" deer came into view.

"Daddy, it's your turn." Marvin said. "You shoot this one."

At the crack of my 243-caliber rifle, the deer dropped.

"Good shot, Daddy," my son congratulated.

At that instant, the deer jumped up and ran out of sight in to a nearby break. (A part of a bayou… it's wet.) Marvin ran to the area and yelled.

"It's dead. I see it, but it's way out there." When I got there, he pointed it out to me. "How are you going to get it?"

I removed my clothes and handed them to him. I waded chest deep about seventy-five yards and had another thirty to go.

"Daddy," Marvin suddenly yelled. "I forgot to tell you that here's a boat!"

I did retrieve the deer, went back to the stand, dressed, and warmed myself by the fire.

Another time Marvin was in a stand by the canal and didn't get to shoot the deer until it was on the other side of the canal. The big question was the same one. How was Marvin going to get the deer?

A hunting buddy, who was also his cousin, heard Marvin shoot just before dark and came to look. It was a really cold day, but Marvin was determined.

"I'll have to dive in and swim across," Marvin informed his buddy.

When he dove, he came up with mud in his face and stood up knee-deep in water. He got his deer.

In the middle of family sport and togetherness, we also shared hurts and struggles. Dorothy Grace graduated from High School without a failing grade at age seventeen. She couldn't get a job until she turned eighteen in November. She applied for a job anyhow. The potential employer read her application with interest until he realized she was only seventeen. In her presence, he ripped it up and threw it in the waste can. This was another chipping away at her self-esteem.

While we were in Deville, both Marvin and Dorothy married. We moved away from Deville, took a church in Winnsboro, and left our two oldest children behind in their new marriages.

Marvin's first wife announced she was leaving the marriage and she took all the households goods as well as the family's finances. I've never seen anyone so traumatized. We did our best to comfort him.

Dorothy gave birth to our first grandson, Randy. We were so proud of him.

Divorce struck again and our daughter distanced from us. During the next few years, this distancing and Dorothy's further struggles brought hurt, not only to her, but also to the family.

We couldn't share our deepest hurts with many people. We were very selective in sharing. But, there were the friends in Kansas who were far enough away and didn't judge.

Marvin's second marriage also ended in divorce, again taking all he had and devastating the finances. His wounds and hurts impacted the whole family.

Dale, the youngest boy, was a different kind of child than the first two. He was easily corrected. At an early age, he was interested in spiritual things. When he was five years old, he gave his heart to Jesus in a revival meeting in Antioch.

About a year later, he came to our bedroom one night and said, "I am going to ask God what He wants me to do with my life."

"He may or may not answer you right away," cautioned him.

The next morning before we got up, Dale was again at our door. "God told me what he wants me to do with my life. He wants me to preach." Because of this early experience, he missed many of the growing up struggles he could have faced.

Dale's growing up years were fairly carefree and good. He has an outgoing nature that draws others to him. He learned to be a 'comedian,' and that brought lots of fun and laughter to life.

He was very selective about his girlfriends. He began dating a girl from the Oak Grove Church that we had pastored.

In 1986, Dale chose to attend Central College, our Church College in McPherson, Kansas. By that time, our friends from the Illinois pastorate had moved to Kansas and the husband was a professor of Aviation and science at Central. Dale's major was Aviation, so he spent much time in their home with ready access to the refrigerator.

When we visited Dale, we found a welcome place to stay in Dick and Cindy's home. Several years later, we received word they had divorced.

After Dale graduated from Greenville College, he married his Oak Grove girlfriend, Cassandra. Dale began pastoral ministry and fulfilled his early calling.

Marvin married a sweet lady named Dorothy, causing the family to adjust and call our Dorothy, Dorothy Grace to keep her and Dorothy Mae straight.

Marvin adopted Dorothy's daughter, Melissa and gave us a granddaughter.

We continued pastoring, and before retiring officially in 1997, we had pastored many of the churches of the Louisiana conference.

In fact, we pastored one church three times at different periods. I remember moving into that same parsonage three times!

Shortly after we retired, Ellen, Dale, Cassie (Dale's wife) and I stopped to see our now single friend, Cindy in Newton, Kansas. We were on our way back from a vacation in Colorado. We had a good visit, and when we went to leave, I questioned her about her happiness.

"Cindy, do you have a boyfriend?"

"No," was her decisive answer. "I'm not looking for one, and don't need one! I'm doing fine without one. God and I are doing fine without one."

Okay. Our single friend was decidedly single!

By 1998, Ellen and I were asked to pastor the Free Methodist Church at Acme, LA. We went down there and enjoyed pastoring the small congregation. I wanted to be closer to the people and build up the church. I came up with the idea of moving the camper down there, and staying in it.

I'd been using it in the woods where I hunted deer, but I'd driven it out of the woods and could now take it down there. Someone in the church had some property close by for us to set it up on.

September 20, 2003 Ellen and I went down there. We were to spend the night in preparation of a homecoming celebration at the Acme church.

Around four in the afternoon, I had hooked up the propane tank to the camper and proceeded to light the gas refrigerator. Then, I had gone into the bathroom to work on the faucets, and heard this loud explosion. And felt it too.

There was this huge blaze that came sailing out through the door, and then Ellen came walking out.

She had a blaze that began at her ankles and went about eighteen inches above her head. She walked all the way past the bathroom door into the bedroom. I followed her.

"I'm burning to death," she said to me.

And the blaze was just roaring. Ellen's clothes were all on fire. I looked around to see if I could find something to smother it out. I saw nothing I could use that way.

My mind was racing for solutions. *"I've gotta do something!"* I thought. *"I can't stand here and let her burn to death....Maybe if I can throw her down on the bed and smother it out."*

And I shoved her down on the bed. To my surprise, instead of helping smother the fire, it caught the bed covers on fire and increased the flame.

"This is not working," I said.

I thrust my hands and arms into the flames and put my hands on her body to pull her off the bed. As I reached for her, her clothes burned off in my hands. I reached in again and pulled more off. Some of the elastic from her clothes burned into my hands. I continued defying the flames and kept pulling, trying to get her out of the camper.

I said one word. "Help!" I was saying it to God as well as to Ellen.

She heard and began to help. With her help, I was able to get her out of the camper. Once outside, we pulled off what clothes that hadn't already burned off. They were still blazing.

She walked about ten feet to the car and got in. And you can believe I burned rubber getting out of there!

My hands were so badly burned even the bones were burned. I drove, though, toward the nearest hospital, thirty-five miles away.

Two miles down the road, I saw a young woman in her yard. I stopped long enough to have her call an ambulance to come meet us as we went toward a little town named Ferriday. The next twenty-six miles were the most horrendous, nightmarish miles I've ever driven.

I would look over at Ellen and cry, "Oh my beautiful Baby." What a horrific moment.

God gave me enough sense to know that I must slow down on the curves and I must be careful when I passed other cars lest I have a head on collision with somebody else.

The ambulance met us, and I made the attendants take Ellen first to begin working with her. I tried to call Marvin, and couldn't get him. So I called Dale and explained what happened. Then I crawled into the cab of the ambulance and gave myself permission to pass out.

I went into a coma.

CHAPTER TEN

REFLECTIONS
MARRIAGE AND MINISTRY
WADE ROBINSON

Favor is deceitful, and beauty is vain: but a woman that feareth the LORD, she shall be praised. Proverbs 31:30

The best thing I ever did in my life was let God take control of my decisions when I gave up Vera. I've said that already, but that encounter has influenced my whole life.

Who wouldn't trade a worn out, beat up ragged Ford Falcon for a shinny new Cadillac? Or a handful of bitter weeds for a bouquet of roses? Or a life in a pig pen with ankle deep mud for a life in a King's quarters?

God's way is always the best, and He provides the best for us when we let him choose for us. This fact was proven to me when I gave up Vera and He brought in to my world a pretty blue-eyed girl who started the bells ringing for me.

I have never been sorry I let God choose for me. Ellen was an asset to my spiritual life and ministry that could not be measured or over looked. She gave me courage when I was discouraged, strength when I was weak, stability when I was unstable.

Beyond that, she was a good mother, and together we taught our children they could know God through Jesus when they were very young.

I am grateful for the forty-six years we had together. She had my heart and my love, and I was always faithful to her.

It also never ceases to amaze me that God was

preparing the way, setting the stage for life many years in the future throughout Ellen's and my life together. He never stopped working in our lives, never stopped planning how best to take care of me even after Ellen was physically no longer with me.

It's awesome how God leads us as we endeavor to follow Him step by step.

Near death experiences and close calls were not a new thing to me. They began when I was two years old and had colitis. I really was very sick, and nearly died.

As a teenager I was riding on the back of a pick-up with a friend. His brother was driving. I had told him I wanted to get off a certain place.

But evidently the driver didn't know it, or forgot or something. When we got to the place

I wanted to get off, we were traveling, I'd say, about twenty-five or thirty miles an hour. I was sitting on the very back of the pick-up with my feet dnagling. It was a dirt road, an dince we didn't seem to be stopping, I decided to jump off.

"Good-by," I said, taking my hands and shoving myself off so I could land on my feet.

But as soon as my feet hit, my rear end hit, and I flipped - I think about three times. It's a wonder I didn't break my back. It did hurt severly. I was able to get up and walk with much pain.

"Are you hurt?" A neighbor who was close by called.

I would not admit it, but yeah, I was hurt. But I never had any treatment for it.

Through the years, I also had a series of near head-on collisions.

When I was pastoring in Chickasaw (the church is now closed) near Olla, LA, I was on my way to the Summerville Camp Ground to help my conference superintendent work on the grounds. A gravel truck was ahead of me. As I attempted to pass the truck, I pulled out into the left lane on a two-way highway.

And to my surprise, there came a vehicle from the other direction. Well, I got on the brakes, and slid, and I couldn't get the car to stop, and it was gaining on the tgruck for a little ways. The on-coming car kept getting closer. Finally, the gravel truck did get further ahead of me. I had pulled the steering wheel to my right.

"I can pull in behind him," I thought as the gravel truck got further ahead of me.

I got off the brakes. The car then jumped to the right side of the road, missing the gravel truck, and missing the oncoming car. I ended up in the ditch without any damage to the car, and none to myself. But it certainly was scary.

Another time, I was on my way to college classes at Greenville, Ill between Litchfield and Hillsboro. It had come up an ice storm that night and early in the morning, I was on my way, and I started up one of the hills. It wasn't a huge hill, but it did have an incline. As I started up the hill, I saw a big truck coming down the hill toward me. And suddenly, the tires on my car lost traction on the road and got in the lane of the oncoming truck. I turned my wheels to the right. But it didn't do any good. I everything I knew to do to get the car back on the right side of the road. But the big truck coming toward me seemed to be the only thing happening.,

As I continued on like that, and the big truck got within two car length of me, suddenly my wheels made contact with the road, the car literally jumped to the side, and the big truck rushed beside me, barely missing me.

The last time I almost had a head-on collli-
sion was between Jonesville and Jena on Hight-
way 84. Ellen and I were on our way to Alexandria. We saw two 18-wheelers coming our way
our way on the highway. Then, suddenly a small
car appeared on my side of the road. It was attempting to pass both the 18-wheelers.

I saw immediately he had not the time or
space. But he continued in my lane. And when he
got within about a hundred feet of me, I whipped
off on the shoulder of the road. And at that time,
he whipped off on the shoulder, and we still continued to come directly toward each other.

*"I have enough room to go between the
18-wheeler and the car,"* I thought.

So I cut the wheel to the left and that's what
I did. I got between the 18-wheeler and the oncoming car. And they whizzed by me. The car
whizzed by on the right side, and the 18-wheel-
ers whizzed by me on the left. I had gone between the car and the 18-wheelers.

I waatched in my rear view mirror as the car
spun out of control and got in the path of one
of the 18-wheelers. The truck hit the car and
knocked it around before they all came to a stop.

I stopped the car and went back. Although the
car was badly damaged, the man was unharmed.
We went on to Alexandria.

******

Hunting has inhernet dangers, but the closest call I had while hunting had nothing to do with guns. My eldest son, Marvin, myself and three other youngmen went out together in Februry of 1980. The temperature was twenty-two degrees that morning, and there was ice everywhere. Their decision was to take boats, our rabbirt dogs, our guns and go to some of the islands where the backwater had pushed the rabbits. They would be plentiful and easy to hunt.

('Backwater' is a condition resulting from excess rain that does not allow the bayous to drain into the river, and everything comes flowing back.)

Well, we got into the boats. I got in with a young man named Eddie Ray, and we had dogs in a crate. I sat in the front with a life preserver and Eddie Ray sat in the back and ran the motor.

Between us was the crate full of dogs. They were literally packed in the crate.

The two guns, my 22 rifle and his shotgun were there by me.

Our boat had a bigger motor, so we could go faster, and we got ahead of the other boat. They were out of sight.

"Do you suppose we should stop and wait for them?" I asked Eddie Ray.

So he cut the motor and the gas. It died. Well, if you know anything about ridding in small boats, you know if you are going any speed, the boat will riase up in the front.

Well, when the boat died, the front was suddenly no longer in the air. It dropped and began taking on water. Then, suddenly, the water was rushing in.

The water was very deep because the backwater was up so far. You could see the tops of tall trees scattered here and there. Off in the distance was a floating duck blind. In the opposite direction was another duck blind. Well, with the boat taking on water like that, I knew it would sink soon.

"Its going to sink! We're taking on water!" I yelled to Eddie Ray.

"Get your life preserver and the guns. I'll let ther dogs out," he called back.

Just as he opened the door to the dog crate, the boat turned over. I did get ahold of the life preserver, and one of the guns. But his expensive shotgun, I missed. It went to the bottom. And I though I was going to go there too.

I was dumped into the water along with Eddie Ray. The dog crate did go the the bottom with all the dogs in it. Not a one of them survived.

I tell you, it was a beautiful sight to see that other boat coming around the bend.

They got us out of the water and we easted over to the nearest duck blind. Marvin pulled off his insulated suit, and I stripped off my wet clothes, which was a mistake. I got colder than I would had been even with my wet clothes on. I put the dry jump suit on and turned blue. Some kind of shock came over my body that stayed with me for a great many hours.

But I thank God the second boat was able to carry us all to the duck blind.

There were other animal encounters that were really dangerous, but I also had some close calls in my work outside the ministry.

I worked with Ellen's brother, Johnny, for a while. He was a man who worked in the pulp woods (mostly young pine trees grown for the purpose of making paper and wood by-products.)

He cut and hauled pulp wood. He hired me to help him load the pulp wood onto his truck.

He had a wench on the truck that would pull the wood, one pience at a time and drag it up to the top of the truck onto the load. And I would operate it.

One day while I was doing that, the pulp wood flipped and changed directions, barely missing me. It could have broken me into pieces.

One time the cable hung on the lever that I was using to operate the wench, and the cable pulled that lever to where it was still on - Even when I had turned loose of it. It continued to draw the cable and pull the pulp wood in. And then, when it got to a certain place, the cable slipped off the handle, and the handle swung with much force within two inches of my head - Right at my forehead. Had it not stopped when it did, it would have burst my head open.

The last time I nearly died working with Johnny happened after we had a load on the truck. We had a chain that goes around the load. When the chain is over the load, it is pulled tight with a thing called a binder. We used what we called a cheater pipe in the last step to secure the load. A cheater pipe is just a length of pipe that slides down over the handle of the binder to pull on for better leverage, so the chain would be tight and hold the load on securely.

Well, I did all that right, except I had the binder too close to the ground and the pipe stuck in the ground. And I needed the pipe off the binder. As I jerked the pipe to get it out of the ground, it caused the binder to trip. "With great force' it came up, out of the pipe, and hit me just below the nose - Between my nose and my mouth - And knocked me backwards. Had it come on-half inch lower, it would have knocked out both my front teeth, and had it hit me one inch higher it would have, according to my doctor, driven my nose back into my brain.

"I'd better not work with you anymore," I told my brother-in-law.

And that ended my work with pulp wood.

But none of the close calls or near death experiences I had in my early life compared to or prepared me for the terrible gas lead and fire on September 20, 2003 that took my dear wife's life and almost took mine.

CHAPTER ELEVEN

POST DIVORCE
CINDY ROBINSON

I took root in Newton, Kansas. Beginning August 22, 1992, God watered, pruned, and fed me as my concepts of Him grew. God and I spent the next thirteen years putting my life into a new order.

But at first, it looked hopeless, really hopeless!

"What was a good Free Methodist girl like me doing DIVORCED?" I wondered. "How many prople could see the big 'D' on my forehead?" The administration of the denomination certainly could since they took my ministerial credentials, and left me devastated once again.

Life didn't wait. It moved on, so I moved into a four-room apartment. I remember the exact address and apartment numbers, and that I lived upstairs four years before moving downstairs. My friend Jean came to my rescue in moving my stuff and helping to get the apartments livable. In fact, she moved me a few times in twelve years.

Later my sister, Ethelyn, and her husband, Melvin stayed with me for a few weeks. They did a lot of fixing up.

The rest of the family was unprepared for my marriage failure.

Ken thought his parent's marriage was perfect. This only affirmed that I had done my job well for many years… my job of hiding secrets, and of wearing a tight smiling mask.

My father was still highly upset with me, and continued to voice his opinion that I had done wrong and that living in an apartment wasn't a good moral thing for me to do.

My mother was hurt, confused, and put much of the blame for my failure on herself. She apologized and asked forgiveness many times. I told she was forgiven, and that I was the one who walked down the aisle.

About this time, Sheryl moved from Kansas back to Illinois, closer to where her dad lived, partly in an attempt to reconcile. Life didn't go well for her at this time. All she could afford was a dumpy trailer clear across town from her job.

Instead of drawing closer to Sheryl, her father met the woman who was to become his second wife and gave her the attention our daughter craved.

Dick's remarriage without any attempt to reconcile stung.

I was rejected, betrayed, misunderstood by friends, and dealing with the lies of Dick's labels, which he no doubt believed were true. Beyond that, I was facing my own sins and failures. That was a pretty heavy ticket.

"What am I doing here, anyway?" I asked myself in the dark one late night driving home from work.

That night I was reading in the Book of Acts and these words jumped out at me, "...he determined the times set for them and exact places where they should live. God did this so that men would seek Him perhaps reach out for Him and find Him, though He is not far from us."

That was answer enough for my troubled soul. Once again I turned my lief over to Him and began that walk to seek Him and reach out for Him.

There were many things I needed to do. I learned how to reconcile a checkbook, take care of a car, and the rest of the practical things about managing an organized life.

Sometime in October of that first year, I drove to Illinois and told my parents the whole story. For the first time ever, I felt Dad cared and was really trying to understand. Since that time, until he died, our relationship healed and he made conciliatory gestures toward me in apologetic moves if not expressing words of sorrow. In ongoing conversations, he affirmed my decisions and realized I had not thrown away my deep-seated values of love and marriage.

After a year and a half away, Sheryl moved back to Wichita, Kansas, about thirty miles south from me. Fortunately, the job she left was still available. She had a desk and a name plaque! God works in mysterious ways....

Life took on a new dimension. I went about enjoying a new job, a new church, and new friends.

With God's help, and the beginning of a new understanding of how He actually works, and how much He loves, God and I set out on a new life adventure.

By January 1993, Ken was assigned to San Antonio, Texas as his Air Force career continued. A few months later, he and his wife were divorced, but they had given me a grandson, Kyle.

Three years later, Ken brought his new-bride-to-be to Kansas to meet me, and I was happy for them. Sheryl and I drove to San Antonio for their wedding. After the ceremony, Ken and Bev changed their wedding finery to motorcycle garb and rode off into the sunset on Ken's motorcycle for a honeymoon! Ken's family expanded as he adopted Bev's two boys. They had McKenna a year later.

Back home, life continued with God giving me friends and opportunities. My daughter and I did the girl things like shopping again. Another friend and I took day trips to relieve stress and get away.

I learned to laugh; to dance. I put together Creative Memory albums for my children, grand-kids, and friends.

I had opportunity to supply the pulpit at Jet (Oklahoma) Nazarene Church. I made history as the first female preacher to preach in the 1st Mennonite Church in Newton, Kansas. I taught a senior citizen's Sunday school class and was the Christian Education director at my new church.

I learned to have fun. I held weekly ladies Bible Study in my home. We were known as the LAMBS (Ladies About the Master's Business).

One Saturday evening, we went to the Garden Café in Wichita. The place was packed and we were given a table toward the back of the seating area. I had been there before and knew one meal was enough for two, and was followed by fabulous desserts.

I told the waitress, who was a fun, young girl, I wanted half-a- meal and dessert. When she came later with the dessert menus, I protested I was much too full.

'You'll have dessert!" she declared and lifted me up out of my chair with a whirl. She hooked her arm around my waist and danced me all the way around the café. Guests were watching, laughing and cheering.

"You are having more fun that we are!" declared the couple in the booth next to us.

Indeed, God planned a very public debut for me into the knowledge that a devout Christian can just be, and have lots of fun. I shared the dessert with the rest of my LAMBS.

In 2001, God gave me a new apartment where I could have family overnight. The new place gave me quiet a boost. It had a wonderful side yard and a place for flowers. It had a built-in row of stately pine trees, which served as a privacy fence bwetween the apartments and the road. There were birds that nested in the treees and gave me a concer in the early mornings as I enjoyed by coffee out-side.

Once again Jean loaded her trusty pick-up truck and moved me part and parcel across town; actually across a set of tracks which separates New from North Newton. There were other church people who pitched in and helped with all the moving details, and I thank God for all of them.

I worked at the Newton Presbyterian Manor, a long-term care facility as part-time social worker and part-time chaplain. Once again in a new place, my life filled up with friends, duties, satisfaction, and meaning.

I developed shopping friends, luncheon friends, Bible study friends, and work friends. With them, I regularly traveled to both Kansas City KS/MO and Wichita, KS. Many times, I traveled alone to Illinois and San Antonio to visit family.

Relationships with my children slowly healed. Sheryl, who by now had a fulfilling career of her own, and I become close friends again. We relied on each other for support. Many times, we traveled to San Antonio together to visit Ken and his family.

By 2004, my life and schedule was full. My 'normal' calendar looked like this:

Every 2nd Monday of the month I had a Chaplain's luncheon.

Every 2nd Wednesday was Ministerial Alliance luncheon.

Every Wed, (except for the second) I had lunch with a couple of girlfriends at the Peace Center, which is a building where people gathered for crafts, meetings and just for 'hanging out.'

Every 3rd Thursday was a Shepherd's luncheon and presentation at Prairie View.

Every other Sunday my Bible Study group, the Lambs, ate together somewhere (in addition to our weekly Bible Study night.)

Added to the standing events were conducting and attending funerals when residents died, office hours, visits with residents, speaking engagement preparation, church work, and occasionally preaching opportunities.

I loved it. Instead of doing church, I was living a life full of work for God's glory. How different it was than those years when I relied on ministry to make me feel whole. Now, ministry was an expression of my growing wholeness, love of, and relationship with a gracious God.

Summer of 2000, my old friends Wade and Ellen Robinson, son Dale, and his wife, Cassie, came through town and we ate together, catching up on each other's lives. When they left, Wade asked if I had a boyfriend.

I repeated what I'd been telling friends and family for some time. "I'm happy with my life. I don't need a man, don't want one, and I'm not looking for one."

Rebirth

By Cindy

Newness, rebirth
Again and again
Old clay broken,
Shattered, cracked
Placed in the Potter's hands
Remolded, reworked, reshaped
To his likeness
Newness, rebirth again and again
Hallelujah.

Breezes

By Cindy

Freshness, breeze blowing
Where it will
Into the dry places of my heart.
"A heart of flesh," He said,
"I will give you."
"Take away my heart of stone," I ask.
Where it will
Into the dry places of my heart.

(Written at a ladies' retreat outside in moments of reflection.)

CHAPTER TWELVE

REFLECTIONS POST DIVORCE
CINDY ROBINSON

By now my whole religious, legalistic form of proving my worth by what I accomplished had cracked, crashed, landed in ruins, and been swept away.

One of my journal entries read: *Pondering... when does one know for sure when one makes a right decision? It seemed right and best. He (Dick) is doing better now – seems to have found new life. Even my Aunt remarked, "He seems to be let out of bondage." She said he was more social and talking more to others. With me, there has been a calm and peace. I don't need to be stoic.*

Another entry is about the 'why?'

"Why couldn't we have had that together? Why did we fail so miserably? He is now doing the things I wanted in a marriage. Makes me darn mad."

Then, slowly I had to put that away too. As my legalistic form of being was being replaced, I had to give that up too.

The legalistic form was replaced as I went from rules to relationships. The transformation took place as I knew for certain God loves me and forgives my sin – right down to the pharisaical attitudes and arrogance. God had to deprogram me from the negative, former system. I learned to let go of perceived importance. I learned to be open with people, and accept them in return. I quit hiding myself from people.

Bad things still happened. In 1997, Sheryl had several hospitalizations that ended in surgery. Her grandparents on her Dad's side treated her unkindly and without compassion over a car sale. In 1998, my nephew, Bruce, died in line of duty training pilots in rescue missions in the California canyons. Somehow, these events didn't shake my foundations, as they would have in the past.

I hate divorce. It is not what God planned. It's hurtful down to the second and third generation. It changes lives forever.

But God is compassionate.

Sometimes marriage, for whatever reason, is not built on mutual trust, caring and unconditional love.

There are marriages in which couples were never friends, in which conflict existed even before marriage.

There are marriages in which partners are already emotionally divorced and living together is a lie.

But God is compassionate.

He was always working to change my life and me.

At thirty, I had two children, a foster daughter, and an emotionally absent husband. I sought to know God, to serve Him. But God, like my well–meaning father, demanded me to be a workaholic, invincible, indestructible, and judgmental, always straining for a standard beyond my reach. Nevertheless, God held me in his hand, protecting me from manifold, lurking dangers.

At forty, I was hurting, alone in the midst of family, rejected, inadequate, inferior, empty, and disillusioned. Yet I wore a plastic smile, worked long hours, never disclosed myself to anyone. But I was there for everyone else, stuffing down the feelings, keeping the lid down tight. I was a Messiah-complex, fixer type person in my church, and conference. "She's a wonderful person," they said, and I cried myself to sleep.

But God is faithful.

At fifty, I became a learner, soaking up new ideas, new insights, and a non-traditional student at college, much to my husband's displeasure and opposition. In spite of it all, God enabled me to become a Social Worker and Ordained Minister. I became a struggling child of God, a person working on wholeness, a recovering workaholic, and a friend of God.

I became a real person – not necessarily always nice – forging out healthy relationships with some balance to my life.

However, I still had an attitude about men! God began to deal with me about it. A counselor once told me not to shut the door on a new relationship as it could be healing. I had successfully shut the door.

God is faithful in the process of changing minds and hearts.

I wrote in my journal January 12, 2004: *"my thoughts go every so often to the possibilities of a man in my life. Most of me says 'it is insanity' but another part says 'why not?' I still have lots of love*
and care to give. I think I know better how to relate in a marriage than I once did. You've taught me so many things in eleven years.

Is there even a man out there who would be interested in my zany life, who would love and accept my family? Is there a man who deeply loves and longs for you? With a sense of humor and love for adventure, willing to love and respect me – is there such a man?

Am I the kind of woman who loves and longs after You, with a sense of humor and love for ad-

venture, willing to love and respect a man – is that who I am? Am I willing to share my life and space with another? Lord, only you know the answers to my questioning heart. If this is at all to be, you alone are God, you alone can put it together, even through e-harmony.com*."*

So, through the encouragement of a friend, I clicked on e-harmony.com – a Christian mating service. I thought that would be safe enough.

I did it partly to send God a concrete message. "I am ready for whatever you have for me."

I didn't get any matches from the service!

The morning of March 3, 2004, I wrote in my journal: *"God, be the manager of my life."*

Yes, I rooted in Newton, Kansas: physically, emotionally, spiritually, and professionally.

March 3rd, 2004 I answered the phone and life changed again.

CHAPTER THIRTEEN

RECOVERY AND RESTORATION
WADE ROBINSON

In the hospital in Baton Rouge, LA where Ellen and I were flown, I roused out of my coma at least long enough to tell Dale I knew I was badly burned, but his mother was worse, and I was afraid she would not make it.

I don't really remember much but two things until three weeks later. But the doctors and family tell me my face and head swelled to the size of a basketball. I didn't look at all like I'd looked before the accident. One lung was completely filled with fluid and the other was partially filled. The doctors didn't give me much of a chance either.

Since our denomination is a connectional church, word of our tragic accident immediately spread. People all over the world began to send up earnest, fervent prayers for the Robinson family. God set a hedge around us all.

The first thing I remember from my coma is that I saw my Daddy. He was a young man ... younger than I remember seeing him in real life. When I roused up a little, I asked, "How's Daddy?" Well, he'd been dead thirty-five years. I can only imagine what the family thought!

The second thing I remember as I was slowly coming out of the coma was once when my caretakers had taken me down to the burn unit. Here they had to scrape off the dead skin. That hurt severely. I don't know to tell you how painful that was. I wouldn't wish that on anyone.

I was still mostly more asleep than awake – or more in the coma than out. I don't exactly how to put that, but I was not yet completely myself.

I remember it seemed I was in a slaughterhouse. The name of it was LaSalle Parish Slaughter House. In that house, beside me were two hogs that had been scraped like you scrape hogs to get them ready for market. I felt like one of those hogs, and I wanted to tell them … "Hey, I'm not dead yet!"

I tell you, it was a terrible thing.

When I awakened completely three weeks after the accident, I asked my sons about their mother. They had to tell me she had died and was buried two weeks earlier.

They also informed me I had skin grafts from my fingertips to my shoulders on both sides of my body. I had large sores on my nose and right ear. My hair was all nearly burned off. My ten fingers were individually wrapped, then wrapped together.

The first chance I had to be alone, I talked to God. "Father, I do not want to be bitter. Save me

from a bitter attitude and let me have a sweet spirit. With your help, I am going to get well!"

From then on, I purposed to take the attitude of
seeing humor in everything I possible could, and
I'd tease anyone I could. My childhood reresolve
from hoeing cotton returned.

"I will get through this." Then I'd get through
the next thing. And then the next.

Humor became a daily quest. For instance,
even though I couldn't walk but a step or two,
they put me in a wheelchair and took me to physical therapy. As the therapist was wheeling me, I
looked at her hands. They were well-manicured
… well, pretty. And I looked up at her and asked,
"Could I borrow your little finger?" Don't forget
the way my fingers and hands were bandaged.

"What did you say?" she asked in surprise.

"Can I borrow your little finger?"

"What do you want to do with it?"

"Well, I need to pick my nose."

Do you know she wouldn't let me use her little
finger!

Well, anyway, after I got out of the hospital
not only my sons took good care of me, but their
wives too. Marvin's wife was wonderful. I have
no complaints on how I was treated.

Marvin and Dorothy Mae took me home with
them, and took care of me. I couldn't shave. They

had to bathe me. They helped with food, dressing, and caring for my wounds. Really, there was very little I could do for myself. I was like a baby. But they took care of me.

After several weeks, with them, I requested to be taken to my own home. And they stayed with me there. My daughter-in-law took me to therapy in a neighboring town five days a week.

Gradually, I felt the pressure of being a burden for my children. And I realized I wanted a wife.

Yes, I missed Ellen. Missed her drastically.

But I needed the things wives do. I needed someone to be with. If I found someone who loved me, she wouldn't mind helping me get well. She could do the things my children were doing for me. They could get back to their lives.

And I needed a companion. I still had lots of love to give.

Ellen told me many times if anything happened to her, I would need a wife. She was right.

I got alone with God, as was/is my custom and began to pray as I contemplated dating again. "Father, I'm very vulnerable here. If you don't help me, I could mess up really badly, and I could be in real trouble. Now, I'm going to be looking for a wife. Help me find the right one. Father, when I ask them (my lady friends) out, and it's not right, cause them to say no."

My next prayer about the subject was, "Who should I see?" And I made a list mentally. My friend in Kansas was on it, but her reply to my question of her need for a boyfriend was so adamant! If I didn't cross her off my list, I put parenthesis around her name. Being a realist, I put her out of my mind as I began dating.

God heard my prayers. All my women friends said no.

With one lady I thought, "I'll sit by her and ask her out." That didn't work out.

When I called another friend to ask her to dinner, she wisely questioned me. "Brother Robinson, how long has your wife been dead?" I told her. "That's too soon," she replied. "I don't want to have a relationship with you that soon."

And so, when we hung up, I just thanked the Lord. Different ones had reasons not to go, and I just said, "Thank you, Lord."

A kind lady did have lunch with me. When I took
her back to her work place, I asked. "May I come and see you?"

"Brother Wade," she replied. "I just don't have time for dating, relationships and all that kind of things." And she went back to her workplace.

And I said, "Thank you, Lord."

With much humor, I shared my attempts to date with Julie, my occupational therapist in Jena, LA. We laughed about the saga, and I recruited the staff in my search for a wife. It was light hearted, but they knew my serious need.

My friend from Kansas kept coming to mind. And she didn't go away.

I shared my thoughts about Cindy with my therapist. Her response was immediate.

"Why don't you call her?"

"The last time I talked to her, she said she didn't want a boyfriend."

"Call her anyway."

Days, even weeks went by as OT continued. And now and again, Julie would prod me.

"Have you called Kansas yet?"

"No."

"You ought to."

"Won't do any good."

"Call."

Then the next day she would say, "Have you called Kansas yet?"

"No."

"Call her."

"Won't do any good."

The next day, I'd start the light hearted conversation. "Well, you going to help me find a wife?"

"Have you called Kansas yet?"

"No."
"Call her."

She and God wore down my fear of rejection. I finally got through it by saying to myself, "The worse she can do is say no. I can handle it."

So, with much trepidation, on March 3, 2004, about 8:45 in the evening, I called Kansas.

CHAPTER FOURTEEN

POST ENGAGEMENT REFLECTIONS
WADE ROBINSON

Ellen had seen something in me that told her even if I were healthy, if she was gone, I would need companionship, help and a wife. And I suppose it was our long, loving relationship that made me long for that again – beyond the physical help a wife would bring.

To all my lady friends' credit, not one of them stated my physical needs as the reason they said no. I think they umderstood the deep void Ellen left in me even though I expressed my needs in physical term. However, I think they knew the big job they would have taken on. They are all wonderful people and continue to be friends.

God is good. He caused Cindy not to say no during that first conversation. She knew about the accident through e-mails that had gone out from our bishops of the church.

In the first phone call, I told her I was alive, told her of my condition, asked about her kids, and told her about mine. At the end of that long conversation, I commented I wished we lived closer than seven-hundred and fifty miles. It was a long distance to just drop in to visit, and I'd like to visit some time. I purposely left that thought with her.

I didn't detect any running away screaming in her attitude. So, two more days of therapy – two longdays – later, I called back.

Somewhere in that long conversation, I could scarcely believe my ears when I heard her words. "Wade, what are you thinking? Where is this going?"

I'm not sure she knew what she was saying, so I clarified. "I want you to be my wife. I have a lot of love to give."

Or something like that. We later confessed to each other we don't really remember our exact words. We talked about Kansas versus Louisiana for a place to live.

"Wade, you've tried to live in the North two times, and both times, after a while you hightailed it back to Louisiana. You won't be happy in Kansas. I'll come to Louisiana."

Just like that. "I'll come to Louisiana."

After the conversation, it took a while before I realized… "I'm engaged." I could hardly wait to tell my family.

I remembered the little poem my Daddy used to say:

Love O love is a thrilling thing
Beauty to its blossom

If you want your finger bit
Stick it to the 'possum

(from the editor: remember the 'possum plays dead and will jump up and unpleasantly surprise you...")

I thought, "I've got the best end of the deal. I was both surprised and elated Cindy said yes.

We both shared our lists.

She shared the list of her requirements, and strangely, I matched all but one. I don't play piano. Of course, if had played, I certainly couldn't play anymore. Cindy reassured me we had cassettes and CD's to play.

It was then I made clear what she was getting into as far as the kind of help I needed. The list read: doctors' appointments, cooking, cleaning house, help me with the Jobst garments (tight fitting elastic type covering for burn patients that helps lessen scaring and promotes circulation.)

It didn't daunt her. Very quickly, she answered. "Wade, I don't cook and I don't clean."

But she didn't change her 'yes' to a 'no.' We negotiated the household tasks, and soon we found a comfortable openness about what we would or would not do. We also found a deep respect and a friendship that blossomed into love.

God was at work. He caused her to say yes."

CHAPTER FIFTEEN

POST ENGAGEMENT REFLECTIONS
CINDY ROBINSON

The personnel of the Manor where I worked in Newton had a field day of humor in the time between the announcement of my engagement and the serious goodbyes.

They didn't mind me getting married, but insisted Wade would have to come north. I knew he'd already tried that.

But they had their fun.

When I forgot a Bible study and had to be called in to conduct it, the group broke into a vocal rendition of "Here Comes the Bride."

Later the wife of a couple came by and said as they watched me return to my office, her husband observed, "Well, she sure has a lilt in her get-along,"

Once I was pre-occupied after making some calls, and went on automatic pilot to home when I should have returned to the office. The explanation of my lateness in returning surfaced when my co-workers discovered I was driving to Louisiana!

My coworkers teased me about driving on to Louisiana! "She will turn the wrong way and end up in Canada!"

An aide who I'd gotten close to informed me she was coming with me and be "the Cajun Mama!"

We had lots of last suppers, laughter, and tears. But friends helped me pack when they realized I was really going away.

In everyone's circle of movement, there are rules to follow in these times of change. In our denomination a divorced person entering the active pastorate, or contemplating marrying a divorced person is required to go through certain channels before they can actively pastor. This is for the pastor and family's protection from disapproval, gossip, or criticism as once the process has gone through the superintendent and Bishops, it cannot hinder the pastor's career in ministry.

So, in the midst of my goodbyes, I consulted with my superintendent. Wade had to do the same as he recovered and prepared for marriage. His assured him there was no problem with me serving in the conference. I suppose he understood where Wade was in life, what he needed, and wanted.

However, like most of my friends, my superintendent was shocked and somewhat wary.

After all, he knew me the past twelve years as a content, settled single!

I told him my story at the beginning and related how God's hand seemed to be at work in the situation. This Godly man had been our pastor when Dick and I were together. Dick told him the problem was all mine.

I described Wade's personality, his love for God and family, how he treated his first wife, his love, respect, and consideration for me and how we would minister together.

"How many men do you know like that?" Superintendent Kendall asked me. At the end of our conversation, he said, "I think God has given you a great gift." He understood and gave approval.

He went on to say the speed of my decision was the thing that probably floored my family and friends. He made me realize I hadn't shared with them the process of the past twelve years or the road I had traveled. It wasn't fair for me to expect them to understand such a 'turn-around.'

No wonder they had reservations and questions!

A very compassionate Hospice Chaplain I worked with gave me confirmation. He had heard me speak, so knew my journey. When he heard of God's work in Wade's and my lives, his eyes filled with tears and he sang out for all the staff to hear.

"Well, Praise the Lord. Hallelujah!"

My friends weren't quite so easy. More than once, I responded to:

"Have you lost your Mind?"

"Have you taken leave of your senses?"

My family's reaction to the way Wade describes looking for a wife was not as positive as my friends. They felt I'd been his last resort, and should have been first. They didn't like the idea of their sister and mother being thought of as a common helper.

"Hey, that's my sister, Bub," was the essence of my Brother's response. Wade took the rebuke with submission and thanked God my siblings showed their love for me.

My children, along with most of my friends, didn't think I'd be happy giving up my career to move to rural Louisiana.

No one knew for sure how I would adjust to a second marriage and a new life. I tried to understand my family and friends' concern for me. However, I had sold out to God's will long ago, and gave Him permission to be my decision-maker. With events of the prior months and changes God had made in me, I believed He gave me a quiet, calm sense of rightness about marrying Wade.

I found in my Bible's margin, a notation next to Psalms 19, "March '04, Louisiana" Verses were 7 & 8 say this: *"The revelation of God is whole and pulls our lives together. The signposts of God are clear and point out the right road. The life maps of God are right showing the way to joy. The directions of God are plain and easy on the eyes."* (The Message.)

At the time I read this passage, it evidently was an affirmation of what seemed a hasty decision I made on March 5th.

So, I came to answer friends and family's questions with:

"Why wouldn't I?" (Be happy giving up my career?)

"Would I deny both of us the privilege and possibility of loving again?"

"Would I deny the possibility of ministry together for Christ?"

"Would I be disobedient to what God wanted me to do?"

CHAPTER SIXTEEN

THE WEDDING
NARRATED BY CINDY ROBINSON

So, both Wade and I, convinced God's guiding hand had joined our winding paths, began negotiating the wedding.

"I want it small." That was Wade in one of our early March '04 conversations.

"Small, but elegant." That was me.

After a second of thought, I asked, "What do you mean by small?"

"Family only."

Not quite. "Family and some friends."

I made him a quick list.

My siblings from Illinois.

My daughter from Wichita, Kansas

My foster daughter and her husband from Wisconsin.

My son and his wife.

Floyd and Nadine (the lilt in the get-along observer).

These 80+ in age friends who I had assisted in their wedding were insisting on driving seven-hundred and fifty -three miles one way to see me married.

The church people who had known Wade "a hundred years."

That would serve as an introduction to most of them, and a bridge between Ellen's friends and me. Ellen's death was just eight months in the past.

Now, Wade doesn't like "big things" or social'todo's." But finally, he agreed.

I turned this "small but elegant" affair over to my daughter-in-law, whose second 'job' is acting as a wedding coordinator. She planned it well. Just what I wanted.

Wade's life has always been filled with love and usefulness and ministry, but not a lot of money. Money for a lot of wedding finery is not something he wanted to put out. But in April my son, his son, their wives, Wade, and I went shopping.

Wade found a really good price on two suits, and was okay with that until the price of the matching shirts, ties and hankies pushed the price beyond his limit. It took him an hour to become okay with it.

"I will never buy another suit!" he declared.

"You won't have to," I quipped. "These will last as long as you live."

But I wasn't that lucky. I ended up buying a dress in Wisconsin when I went to attend my grandson's college graduation.

Wade had a cold and some fever on the evening of the rehearsal. Besides not feeling well, he wasn't happy with all the 'hoop-te-do."

He really wanted to make me happy, or we wouldn't have gotten that far. He said once when he and Ellen got married, "All I did was show up at the church for the wedding."

But he knew this was important to me – so he did his best. Before we were to go to the fellowship room for pizza after the rehearsal, I found him alone in the back of the sanctuary.

"Whaat's the problem?" I asked. "You don't look like a happy groom."

We had a short conversation, duly noted by the families, I'm sure. He didn't feel totally accepted by some of my family, and it was just too much.

"I thought you said small?" By the time we finished the conversation, he apologized. "I'm sorry, I'm ruining it for you." His extra effort lightened his mood, and he entered into the festivities.

It touched me. He really cared if I was happy.

May 29th was a bit windy, but beautiful. Hair appointments and stuff took up the morning.

The 'small group' arrived - The expected ones, plus my ninty-three year old mother, a niece with her three children and my siblings, all from Illinois.

Wade still felt bad. The fever had gone, but he wasn't symptom free. I felt badly for him.

In addition to Wade's cold, I knew there was an undercurrent of disapproval and tension in a lot of people.

My family still wasn't sure I knew what I'd done and was doing. Wade's extended church family and some colleagues weren't certain he'd waited long enough for a new, healthy relationship to have a good chance. And who was this woman? And where did she come from?

Ellen's family was a beautiful bright spot. Her brother and sister readily sang for the ceremony. They were already calling me 'sister.'

And I knew this was the man God had hand picked for me. And Wade was convinced I was God's choice - Because of his specific prayer "Make (lady friends) them say no, if it's not right."

So, in spite of everything, I put it all aside and gave myself to the ceremony. It went well.

When we were introduced as Rev. and Mrs. Wade Robinson and it was time to start down the aisly, a loud, heart-felt, celebratory, "Hallelujah!" split the air. The congregation responded with spontaneoul laughter and hilarity. I recognized the voice of my niece, who is a fun and loving person. It made the day, and broke the tension in my soul.

Not the best of beginning: somewhat shaky with mixed feelings and motives. I would not advise it for anyone!

However, if you "know because you know, because you know..." that it is God, and to still *not* be obedient would *not* the thing to do!

CHAPTER SEVENTEEN

REFLECTIONS ON THE PRESENT
Cindy and Wade Robinson
And Interview with Jo Bower

What is the best, unexpected thing about your re-lationship?

CINDY:

Wade's spontaneity and love. At any time, he may burst into song - or prayer. He tells me many time a day that he loves me. He looks for ways to please me. He learned quickly what I like (water, no ice, with lemon!). And what I don't like.

He doesn't compare me with Ellen and I somewhat feared that.

One great thing is that almost from the first, we would both be thinking of the same things at the same time. That continues. It's uncany, almost like we've been together for years. Our spirits are kindred. We laugh at the same things - the same kinds of things make us glad or sad. For two people, different gender and definitely different cultures, we were tuned in from the start.

WADE:

I got a very loving mother-in-law that came with the package. I didn't know she was that precious. And most of the family members went out of their way to make me welcome.

I don't know how to put this into words, but I found Cindy more able to respond to my physically than I thought she might because of her previous marriage.

Cindy accepts all my idiosyncrasies and awkward ways. She doesn't chew me out.

What is the worst unexpected thing about your relationship?

CINDY:

Early on, March '04, prior to marriage, Wade said "I have one pace .... slow. I said, "I have one pace .... fast." So, it is an ongoing challenge for me to slow a bit for him, and him to hustle a bit. Generally, we meet in the middle. Wade is always patient with me and I am learning patience with him.

One of the worst things for me was getting used to living in another woman's home, using her kitchen, sleeping in her bed, with 'her' husband. I didn't realize I'd be my own worst enemy and compared myself with Ellen until God showed my Romans 12:9. *Love from the center of who you are; don't fake it... Be good friends who love deeply; practice playing second fiddle*
.

(The Message)

When I read that, I bowed my head in tears and offered up to God all my frustrations of being a second wife. Earlier in the chapter the author of Romans talks about all being parts of one body. Ellen did her part, and I'll do mine.

Although Wade missed Ellen, he freely gave himself to me, emotionally as well as sexually. He reassured me, praised me, and he gave me compliments and attention. He told me whenever he thought of Ellen, he purposely turned his thought to me. When he cried, I was there for him, and when I cried, he was there for me. We've never turned away from each other in grieving times.

WADE:

It seems that I was not accepted by some of Cindy's family.

What about the relationship makes you laugh?

CINDY:

The ludicrous notion of a fast paced, independent, assertive, self confident, Yankee female
voluntarily relocating to the South and marrying a dyed-in-the-wool Southerner, who is a slow paced, deliberate, determined, male still in the grief process for his first wife!

Our relationship is full of laughter, tears, feelings, trust, understanding, and sometimes misunderstanding, which is quickly resolved.

How do I say that Wade's love for me is enhanced by his love for everyone? He makes connections with everyone he meets. He asks clerks
"Do you take out on town cash?" He does it to get their attention. Then he can pursue a conversation with them. He may leave a Wal-Mart cashier by saying Merry Christmas any month of the year. He gets people to smile and laugh. He doesn't just do business – he spreads cheer and gives of himself. And he gives cheer and laughter to me.

WADE:

Here is an example of the typical things we laugh about:

Early Friday morning, September 23, 2005, we paid twelve doaars to replace our auto registration because we couldn't find the original. About thirty minutes later I asked Cindy where it was. We were traveling to Farriday (a small neighboring town) to make her Hospice calls. She looked in the glove box where she thought she put it. We had already made on stop at the bank and did some business there before we missed it. Comdu called there to see if they found it. No. So, during the day, in the car we emptied the glove compartment four times, goive through every itme and piece of paper. We emptied Cindy's purse three times, and checked under every seat and places in the car. It was no where to be found.

So, we went back to the Driver's License place around three forty-five, and we were going to pay another twelve dollars for a second copy. The computers had already been shut down for the day. But the lady gave us a statement saing we tried to get one. During the whole, frustrating time we laughed and joked about what Cindy had done with the paper. She was sure someone was out to get her.

We finally got home about four PM. There was a message from the man who did the car inspection at nine o'clock in the morning! He said I'd left the paper on his desk! We immediately drove back to town and picked it up.

We've laughed and teased because I was so sure I handed Cindy the registration, and she was just as sure she had put it in the glove box. Like other things, it will become a loving inside joke ... "Cindy would you look in the glove box and make suire we have that registration?" We have many inside jokes.

CINDY:

If anything now is missing, it's "Cindy, did you look in the glove box?"

What are the challenges in your relationship?

CINDY:

Wade's hearing. I tend to talk fast and then he can't understand what I say. I'm learning to slow down, talk clearer, and help him understand. We've had some humorous exchanges until I've repeated something a time or two.

We disagree about tips at a restaurant. Wade is more conservative with money than I am due to his background and being poor. After a couple of times I was pretty unhappy with his tip, so now after the meal he takes the bill to go pay while I leave the tip.

As conservative as he is about money, the first thing he did when we left the church after the wedding ceremony was to put his checkbook in my purse.

"It stays there," he said.

He takes it out to pay bills and then puts it back in the purse.

When I ask a question or we are discussing something, he needs time to think! Generally, I pop off the first thing that comes to mind. He doesn't. I'm learning to be quiet and wait until he has formulated his answer and is willing to share it.

"Make do' is his motto. Mine is "replace it." We've learned to compromise with one another.

And I'm learning to cook again, and be in a relationship with another person.

WADE:

The way we spend money. I've about surrendered to the fact that when it's all gone, and we hit bottom, we'll deal with it.

It's also a challenge to see what we could consolidate. How to take the best of two households, use them, and let the rest go.

Another challenge for me is how to express the grieving process in a healthy manner. I "go through the fire" every day. Sometimes it's intense enough that the tears come unbidden. I never want to hurt Cindy. Instead, I've learned she willingly give me comfort and encourages me to share the experience with her. When does remembering and grief end? Maybe never totally, but meantime, we are partners in the grief process ..... I'm getting better with time.

Tell me about your families now.

CINDY:

Ken lives with his wife, Beverli in San Antonio,
Texas. He is retired from the Air Force, and is now
Vice President of Operations in the Vital Needs International Corporation. His hobbies include biking, photography, ham radio operator, and reading.

Bev works as a consultant and Coordinator for
events, with her specialty being weddings. She creates custom Christmas decorations for commercial properties. She likes to entertain, plan big events, attend her children's football games, track meets, marching contests, and take her daughter shopping.

They have four children: Drew, Kyle, Cade, and McKenna.

Sheryl lives in Wichita, KS. She has a cat, Callie, who is a family member – just ask Callie! Sheryl is a Team Leader for ComCare for Wichita, and manages several Case Managers. She also works part time at Target. She is involved in her church and with her friends.

Her hobbies are piano and reading, as well as gadgetry!

Connie lives with her husband Leroy, formerly of Jefferson, WI. Recently they joined Wycliffe Translators and plan to spend a year in missionary work.

They have two sons; Andy and Rob.

Connie's hobbies are gardening, quilting, reading, biking, kayaking, and scrap booking. Leroy's hobbies include biking, kayaking, and reading.

WADE:

Marvin lives with wife, Dorothy Mae in rural Jonesville, just a hundred yards or so from us. He is an Officer at the Catahoula Correctional Center. His hobbies are hunting and raising rabbits and chickens.

He has a stepson, Keith Adams and a daughter, Melissa. Dorothy Mae is a top-notch homemaker and loves garage sales.

Dorothy Grace lives with her husband, Wayne in rural Belah, LA. They love to garden and be outdoors. She is an excellent cook and homemaker. She loves to bake bread. Her son, Randy, attends McNeese State University in Lake Charles,

LA. She sums up her life with these words: "I am happier than I have ever been." Wayne writes songs, plays guitar, and is a professional painter. His work is pretty awesome.

Dale lives with his wife, Cassandra, in Deville, LA. He is a Free Methodist Minister, as well as a licensed Plumber. Cassie is an Administrative Assistant for Metal Roofing Manufacturing. They have two children, Katie Marie, 16 months and Travis Dale, jr, 2 months old. They have a busy household. Dale loves to hunt and Cassie is an avid scrap booker.

CINDY:

I'd like to add a word about Ellen's family. When they knew Wade was marrying me, they started calling me Sister. Her nieces call me Aunt Cindy. I could never think of Wade cutting off any relationships with her family. They were his family for forty-six years. Now, by their open acceptance, they are my family too.

It is also heart warming that on Wade's side of the family, I am also called sister by his only living sibling, Lillian, and his nieces and nephews call me Aunt Cindy.

God is faithful to give me a large, extended family in addition to my own family – maybe a foretaste of heaven!

How would you sum up your relationship?

CINDY:

I know it sometimes sounded like Wade was looking for a wife/servant he wanted to do this and this and that. But, he gives more than I do.

He often vacuums the floor, helps with the cooking of dinner, and hangs clothes on the line. He knows how to make biscuits and scramble eggs, and make waffles. I've learned to cook again. He hates the smell of it, but makes my morning coffee anyway. He brings me cold water to drink. He is so attentive to my needs.

He sings to me and jokes and laughs with me. He teaches me about the trees, the flowers, and all the little southern critters around and their natures.

He studies me and works to be a good husband.

By the time I got here, he didn't need much help. Bandages were off. I help with buttons – the small buttons on his shirt. But that's about all I do any more. He is a great loving man, and we serve each other with love.

My youthful dream was to have a marriage relationship based on mutual love, understanding and unconditional acceptance – one in which we would laugh and cry together, serve God together, share devotions and grow spiritually together. It didn't happen.

Fifty years later, it is happening. We do these things. We have a unity, a harmony, as well as the times we disagree or misunderstand – neither of us uses the phrase "I told you so…" Both freely and willingly say, "I'm sorry – will you forgive me?"

Wade is in tune with both god and my spiritual needs and God. He prays with me at the drop of the hat. We pray together daily. When someone calls and has a prayer request, we stop right there and we pray together.

We are in tune with one another spiritually. And we can share that. We read books together and discuss them. It's just a great relationship. One that I never ever dreamed I would ever have.

Even the grieving process has brought us closer together. In fact, we both went and are going through the grieving process.

Wade grieved for life as he knew it and missing Ellen, who had been his best friend as well as wife for forty-six years.

Me, I grieved for my close-knit friends. I grieved for leaving my daughter in Wichita, for the regular times we shopped, went to movies, and ate together. And I grieved for some of my family members who found it very difficult to accept that I would take on a southern way of life to marry a poor, country boy.

So, Wade and I comfort each other and in doing so found our love for one another growing deeper. The relationship has been and is, in my opinion, learning new dance steps with God leading the dance.

Sometimes it's a waltz, sometimes a good ole' country hoe down. Sometimes the dips, turns and swirls of a fast dance (I don't know names of dances!). Always with the same partner, one who is continually letting go of the past and looking to the present and future with me. It is absolutely great.

Wade's personality is somewhat represented in this scenario the evening of a surgery on his right hand. I gathered the necessary supplies the nurse had given me to squirt water out of a syringe into the palm of his bandaged hand.

He saw what I was about to do and said, "You will not."

"I will too," I answered.

"No you won't." It was a bit louder.

"Yes I will," I asserted, getting frustrated.

Now he was getting determined. "No, you are not supposed to put water down into a bandaged hand."

Frustration got the best of me. "Wade, you were asleep. I wasn't when the nurse told me to do this."

"You're not going to do this."

"Yes I am."

Suddenly a light bulb switched on in my head. I handed him the paper with the phone number of the hospital and said. "Call the nurse and find out for
yourself."

After a brief conversation with the nurse, he sat
back down at the table, stretched out his hand.

"Do it to it."

Wade stands up for what he believes is right, but if proven wrong, he's the first to say, "I'm wrong, I'm sorry."

He truly lives 'in honor, preferring one another" in our marriage relationship.

And I love him.

WADE:

I'm glad Cindy came down here. I want her here. I like what we have. What more could a man want?

Cindy is all I want in a woman. I told Cindy for weeks that I was looking for a rose and God gave me an orchid.

Then just before the wedding, the florist came with the flowers. We overheard her apologizing to Beverli, Cindy's daughter-in-law.

"I'm sorry the roses just didn't look good. I hope you don't mind that I substituted an orchid."

That affirmed what I said all along.

God has blessed us with a very strong and good marriage. Love has grown very quickly and very deeply.

And we look for ways to show love to one another.

CINDY:

How do we say how this relationship really is? Family members on both sides felt this marriage was one of convenience, and on my side, they feared Wade would use me.

But some time in nearly every day Wade hugs me and says, "Thank you, Darling, for coming!" Then wherever we are, sometimes just after we've gone to bed, I'll hear him say, "It (the Bible) says 'ask and you will receive', thank you Lord for answering my prayer. Thank you for this beautiful woman. Thank you for not letting me mess up." (Now, I *am* aware that beauty is in the eye of the beholder!) He is so spontaneous with his praise, sometimes not directly to me but in a prayer to God in my hearing. Completely non-using, and non self-serving.

Who knows what life will bring - the story goes on, never boring, never routine, always an adventure...but that's how God works!

A Final Thought
From Cindy Robinson

At the time of this writing, Wade is still in the process of recovery. Occupational therapy in Natchez, Mississippi continues. He has had elevan skin grafts, and, after two years he is beginning to see the end of the recovery process.

Also, as we were writing this, I realized the Hunsaker family, which was not close through the growing up years, is experiencing a new closeness now. When my brother, Lowell, and I talked about the writing of this book, we disagreed on some things, even the writing of it.

But he said to me, "Whatever you do about it, you will not alienate me from you. You are my sister. Janet and I are about family."

That sums it up for my siblings and I. We are family.

My mother is ninety-four years old and still experiencing personal growth. She is quick with her praise of any of her children, and reaches out to touch and love them. She is about her children, praying for them daily and showing the love that was difficult to do through the years. She remembers every child, grandchild, great-grandchild, and great-greatgrandchild by name in prayer every day. Today "Everybody loves Jewel" still.

Dad died August 25, 2001. At his memorial service, the church was filled to capacity, scarcely even room to stand. The pastors of the conference nearly raised the roof singing "When the Saints Go Marching In." There were *Amen's* and *Hallelujahs* freely expressed. You see, for several years prior to his death at age 92, he invested energy, time and love into all he met. He took garden produce and fruit from his fruit trees to shut-ins and to all his neighbors and friends. He held many grand and great-grandkids on his knee and entranced them with his stories. He was proud of his children and learned compassion at their failures. Time heals wounds. Time changes people. ***It is never too late!***

"...Despite all these things, overwhelming victory is ours through Christ, who loved us..."
Romans 8:37
(New Living Translation).

Happily Ever After......
May 2011
Adjustments and The Grief process
By Cindy Robinson

Happily Ever After......
May 2011
Adjustments and The Grief process
By Cindy Robinson

My mother is now in heaven, the place she longed for in the 6 years after dad died. With victory she laid her earthly burdens down and left her torch for us to carry on. Before she died, she expressed gladness and joy over her new son-in-law Mother stayed with us a couple of months the last summer she lived. She hadn't been here long when Wade called me aside. He said, "You need to say, 'yes, ma'am' and 'no ma'am' to your mother." I told him if I did she would wonder if I was ill. This was not at all the custom in Yankee country. So the blending of two cultures began.

After the wedding on May 29, 2004, the good times and the not so good times were on a roll. There were many challenges for us. I was indeed living in the country, adjusting to another person who still grieved for his first wife.

I wore two hats, that of a caring Social Worker, trying to be a part of the process and the other hat of a new wife who loved and cared for a husband. Sometimes the roles were all confused into one another.

Sometimes, in my desire to be helpful, I overstepped my bounds into Wade's deep hurt where I didn't need to be. Sometimes I felt like an intruder in his grief and experienced guilt at me being alive and Ellen wasn't.

We both had a truck load of losses and oft times, I wondered how this was going to work. Except for God's love and grace, it couldn't. Wade not only grieved his first wife, but his camper and all the things in it; the loss of his self-image, now burned and struggling to button his shirt and not being able to do many things that he used to do.

His fire experience was such a trauma; he experienced flashbacks and continues to have them, though not nearly so often. It *was* such a horrible thing to wake up in the middle of the night yelling in agony, reliving the fire. During those horrible experiences, was I a wife or a Social Worker trying to see him through them? Often I wasn't sure.

In my journal on 12-29-04, I wrote, "I'm beginning to realize Wade may always have times of reliving the fire, times of pulling Ellen out of the fire, times of missing his life with her.

Without the grace of God these times would hurt much worse than they do. I am learning to make peace with it – trying to accept it as a normal grieving process."

I couldn't fault Wade his grief, I suffered my own. I left a daughter in Newton, KS and missed the times we had together. I lost the easiness of relationship with some of my family members who are dear to me. I left my place, my profession, and many of my Kansas friends, as well as parted with some stuff that carried fond memories; I "garage-saled" most of my possessions. Why is it when one moves, relationships change? It is sad and I cried! Wade cried! However we both had a deep belief God put us together to serve Him, to love one another, to serve others in ministry together and to make a difference in lives we touch. God made us a team to do His work with what time we have left in this world.

With that as my mantra, God helped me keep my focus even when I was unsure of my place as Wade's wife. New family and friends I met here were gracious in the early days (and continue to be). Ellen's brother Paul calls me Sister; her other siblings do as well; one of Ellen's best friends told Wade she was "proud" he had me and gives me hugs.

The strangeness of a new culture melted away as Ellen's family and friends reached out to me and drew me in. Tension was less also as I let them know they didn't have to drop Ellen's name or memories from conversation. They were free to talk about her in my presence; after all she was a part of Wade's life for over 46 years. One doesn't chop off one's history. I found online this portion of a poem by Omar Khayyam of Iran (1048 -1131) which Wade and I apply to the histories of our lives (although Wade had quoted it to me many times) :

The Moving Finger writes; and, having writ,
Moves on: nor all thy Piety nor Wit
Shall lure it back to cancel half a Line,
Nor all thy Tears wash out a Word of it.

I would be much less than what God wanted me to be if I bristled at the mention of her name. Our marriage began with all these challenges. In just a week, our church family camp began.

That meant many people over the conference to face and get to know. These were now my people. Before we arrived on the camp ground, Wade told me he was sorry but we would have to share an outside bathroom with others.

That is strange; that was *in* years past church campers had to do that, but I didn't question. When we took our stuff into the cabin, I looked around and noticed an indoor bathroom, with shower. I quickly told Wade, "We are in the wrong cabin; there is a bathroom in here." He went along with me for just a little bit.

Then I saw him smiling and his eyes crinkling around the edges and knew I'd been had! That was the first of many times of "pickin" as I learned these Southern folk do with flair!

Then we made our way to walk around the camp and Wade introduced me to his friends; friends who knew about the death of his first wife. Also they were Ellen's friends; they loved her and missed her.

Then one dear lady, when introduced to me, said to Wade, in surprise, "I thought we would come to camp to comfort you and here you already have a new wife."

Okay, I knew this lady meant well, however I swallowed hard and fought tears. How long would I live in Ellen's shadow? It wasn't long until this friend and I were friends, gave hugs and were glad to see one another.

Isn't God good? His grace and mercy are always plentiful when we need them.

It was during this camp week on the last day; Dale knocked on our cabin door about 5 am and said, "We are going on to the hospital."

WOW. We were up and around; our new little grandchild was coming!

Now Wade was still learning to button his shirt and I generally waited as he struggled with it. It was good therapy for him. However on this morning, there was no waiting; I did the buttoning and we hurried to Rapides Hospital, about 30 minutes away.

We waited and we paced; we prayed and we snacked….all day. Both sides of the family gathered and speculated. Finally Katie Marie Robinson was born. So within 14 days of my new marriage I became a new Gran Gran, much to my delight.

(Thirteen months later her brother, Travis Dale Robinson, JR was born at the same hospital. Same scenario, family members of both sides praying, laughing, talking, waiting and finally Travis came into the world.

What a joy he is to this Gran Gran. God knew I didn't get to be geographically close to my biological grandchildren so he provided these for me. What an awesome God.)

Just a few days into the marriage, one sunshiny morning, I put breakfast on the table. Wade went into the kitchen and pulled the window shade all the way down. I flew into him with a vengeance.

I said, "Of all the things here I enjoy, one is the early morning sunshine coming in the East window. And you come in here and pull the shade down and shut it out!"

He was flabbergasted and finally said, "But, Baby, when I sit at the table, the sun is in my eyes." Oh my, I was contrite. So I put the shade back down. After breakfast I asked him to put it back up!

We had so many things to learn to accommodate one another.

I soon learned Wade was a very frugal shopper. We went grocery shopping together for several weeks. I had no clue how to cook southern cuisine! I didn't know what to buy. I was used to eating wheat bread (could hardly abide white bread, that balled up in a doughy knot in the stomach) so I purchased it.

After some months of this Wade finally spoke up and said he wanted "light bread." I had never heard that term so he explained it was white bread!

Oh no! He was patient and I continued to buy wheat bread. Finally one day in the grocery store, we were in the bread aisle.

Suddenly he picked up a loaf of cheap white bread and threw it in the cart. I asked him what that was all about. He said, "I'm sick and tired of brown bread." So we began to buy both.

After this many years together and with the support of Wade's Doctor, Wade now eats brown bread. At one point in a Doctor visit, Wade was empathically told, "You start eating Yankee food; the Southern food is killing you." I didn't want Wade to die and Dr. Chaudhry supported my cause to eat healthy!

Wade really tried to change eating habits. It didn't always work. One day I *baked* fish. Everybody knows in the South fish is deep fried! Wade took a couple bites, pushed back his plate and asked, "Where is the peanut butter?"

We always keep peanut butter on hand for these occasions; now he eats more real food and less peanut butter! Wade's motto is: I can't have salt, I can't have sugar - if anything tastes good, I need to spit it out.

One day when the family gathered for fried catfish, French fries and hush puppies, I also put on a bowl of cooked green beans.

The Robinson children *tried to tactfully* explain, "Ma, we don't have green beans when we have fried fish!" We all had a good laugh and I quit wasting the green beans on fried catfish day.

In the first months here, I learned to save money by hanging out clothes on wash day. I didn't mind the time then (I seemed to have more of it in the beginning), and I did so much enjoy watching the skies and the clouds and all their interesting shapes. I enjoyed listening to the frogs croak and the birds singing, all different notes and sounds.

I liked the country, the breeze gently blowing in my face, watching the trees sway and the warmth of the sunshine! The clothes always smelled so fresh. One day my clothes were on the line and some birds flying over decided to use them for their bathroom! That did it. I began to use the dryer.

I had only been married a few days when one morning as I was getting breakfast ready, I heard a terrible clacking outside the carport door. I couldn't imagine what sort of southern critter was out there. I yelled for Wade. He came and listened. He patiently explained, "Baby that is a Mongoose. They make that kind of noise. But they are so fast you won't be able to see it."

I looked out the door anyhow and didn't see anything. With a degree of uncertainty I looked up mongoose in the dictionary. It said a mongoose was an agile ferret size mammal mainly from India!

Once again, I'd been had! Wade was laughing and the thing sounded off again so he showed me outside the door was a little green blob about the size of a nickel. I learned about tree frogs.

The learning wasn't all fun and games. One morning at breakfast I opened a pint jar of candied pears I found on the shelves. Wade offered prayer then I noticed his tears. I asked what *was* the matter. He said Ellen had canned those pears "last summer," which would have been not long before she died. My heart sank. Again, I didn't fault his grief but I begged God for wisdom and grace to know how to handle these times. I took the jar of pears off the table and made a mental note to not use any more of Ellen's canned goods. Other friends were recipients of her labors.

Of course there were the times in conversation with others Wade would refer to me as "Ellen." Sometimes in prayer he would inadvertently pray for me calling me Ellen. Sometimes I would quietly say, "My name is Cindy," and he would be so sorry. Other times he never realized it and I didn't say anything.

Quietly I looked to the Lord who supplied the grace. It is a good thing I wasn't too fussy about it because the day came when so naturally I referred to Wade as "Dick," my former husband's name. Ouch, I was done in! How very embarrassing. Rather than make these hurtful times of blaming and judging they became times of growing together in greater understanding.

Wade never made it difficult for me by comparing me with Ellen; not even when I messed up good food because I didn't know how to cook it "southern." I began to compare myself. Ellen was a great cook. I hadn't cooked much in my 12 single years and certainly not with the southern seasonings and flair.

I learned in retrospect, Northern food can be very bland*!* Ellen was also a great seamstress. She had experience from a very early age; she worked in a garment factory at one time. I had a sewing machine so I could mend rips and *do* hems. Sum total of my sewing!

When Wade wanted something done, he soon learned to get the machine out and do it himself. Sometimes I felt like a failure. The yard showed evidence of Ellen's handiwork; she loved flowers. I love flowers also but never had any luck with them. So I racked up my shortcomings stacked alongside the things she did well.

One day I wondered where I fit in this marriage. It happened we were in Natchez for Wade to have Occupational Therapy (which we did sometimes 5 days/week). For the hour he was occupied I took my Bible and journal to a nook in the hospital where I could get quiet.

On this day I was reading in Romans 12 where Paul explained about the body of Christ; we all have our part to do and can't function without one another.

The clincher came for me when I read verse 10 in <u>The Message</u>, "Practice playing second fiddle." Ouch, I bowed my head and cried out in prayer for God to take away any unChristlike feelings I might have hidden within me. This began the real journey of losing myself in order to really accept myself.

On November 11, 2004, I wrote in my journal, "I thought a lot about Wade today. He is such a blessing to me. I know God sent me to Louisiana not only to be a wife to Wade but to teach me some lessons about mutual submission, waiting with cheerfulness and about intimacy, not only with Wade but also with God. Wade is a precious husband – so thoughtful of me…"

December 12, 2004 "Wade has taught me so much about life, about love, about waiting, about understanding and about knowing there may never be resolution to some things. Total healing may come on the other side."

Another journal entry of 1-6-05 "I wouldn't be honest if I didn't tell of the tears I cried early on when I first married, tears of grief for myself always filling 2nd place, tears of not feeling at "home" in my home, tears of feeling competition with Ellen.

But God's grace has held me steady and taught me more about His Body. I am only a part of it – so was Ellen. But I am working to move out of her shadow and find a place of my own in Wade's heart.

I know he tries so hard to be all to me that he can possibly be. He studies me, learns my habits, what pleases me, and generally how to make me happy. What a gracious man!"

Finally in my journal, 1-28-05 "Ouch, Lord, help me to cease longing and stressing for family approval. It is so very important to me but I can't control how they think and feel about me. I need peace – need to let it all go. I relinquish them to you. And I thank you for calling me to Wade and to Louisiana. Thank you for bringing me a husband who is my closest, intimate friend, that we delight in each other; he is so real, so caring toward everyone, enjoys all of life while he recovers from burns. I can't even describe this man who has so many exciting and wonderful sides to him, so willing to share, to give comfort to those who hurt. He laughs with those who laugh and weeps with those who weep. He deeply loves you and deeply loves me. I want no one else. Help me find rest from this burden that's been so heavy. Maybe it was needed so that I would surrender deeply to you and that I would consider the cost of my actions and know I made the right decision. I am content. I am happy here. I am at home."

Mitch Albom wrote in his book <u>Tuesday's With Morrie</u>, "As long as we can love each other and remember the feelings of love we had, we can die without ever really going away. All the love you created is still there. You live on in the hearts of everyone you have touched and nurtured while you were here. Death ends a life not a relationship."

I learned this even more in a conversation with Wade one day. Something was mentioned about Ellen and I said, "I know you loved her." Without batting an eye, Wade corrected me, "I love her."

That stung and tears welled up in my eyes. He said, "Baby, my mama died 34 years ago and I love her; my daddy died 37 years ago and I love him. Your daddy died a few years ago, do you love him?" Point made. Mitch Albom was right. Wade was right. God's love is forever and our love for one another is eternal. How liberating is that!

In the early months and years of our marriage, God taught me some tools to be "ok" with Wade's grief.

1. Distance emotionally and know his grief is HIS grief.

2. Snuggle up to God and remember he is my first love

3. Open up to Wade and allow him to talk about it without any defensiveness on my part.

4. Try to understand his perspective.

5. Accept Wade for all he is.

As I close this chapter, I have to say Mr. Albom is right, God put us here in relationships to love and to learn from one another. These don't change just because we changed the places we live, either on earth or in heaven.

How amazing, one day Wade and I both will meet Ellen again; meanwhile we live, laugh and love to carry on God's message to the world – Jesus is the All-sufficient One who knows what He is doing in our lives. He longs to save us, to reconstruct us and to walk along beside us.

www.ingramcontent.com/pod-product-compliance
Lightning Source LLC
LaVergne TN
LVHW051626080426
835511LV00016B/2203